Field Guides to Finding a New Career

Nonprofits and Government

The Field Guides to Finding a New Career series

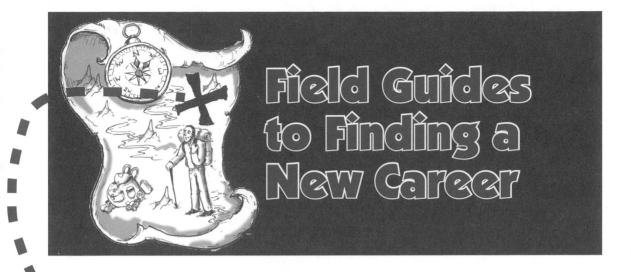

Nonprofits and Government

By Amanda Kirk

Checkmark Books®
An imprint of Infobase Publishing

Field Guides to Finding a New Career: Nonprofits and Governments

Copyright © 2009 by Print Matters, Inc.

Checkmark Books
An imprint of Infobase Publishing
132 West 31st Street
New York NY 10001

Library of Congress Cataloging-in-Publication Data

Kirk, Amanda.
    Nonprofits and government / by Amanda Kirk. — 1st ed.
        p. cm. — (Field guides to finding a new career)
    Includes bibliographical references and index.
    ISBN-13: 978-0-8160-7604-8 (hardcover : alk. paper)
    ISBN-10: 0-8160-7604-9 (hardcover : alk. paper)
    ISBN-13: 978-0-8160-7628-4 (pbk. : alk. paper)
    ISBN-10: 0-8160-7628-6 (pbk. : alk. paper)
1. Nonprofit organizations—Vocational guidance—United States.
2. Administrative agencies—Vocational guidance—United States.
3. Civil service positions—United States. I. Title.
    HD2769.2.U6K58 2009
    331.7020973—dc22

                                                        2009000600

Checkmark Books are available at special discounts when purchased in bulk quantities for businesses, associations, institutions, or sales promotions. Please call our Special Sales Department in New York at (212) 967-8800 or (800) 322-8755.

You can find Ferguson on the World Wide Web at http://www.fergpubco.com

Produced by Print Matters, Inc.
Text design by A Good Thing, Inc.
Illustrations by Molly Crabapple
Cover design by Takeshi Takahashi

Printed in the United States of America

Bang PMI 10 9 8 7 6 5 4 3 2 1

This book is printed on acid-free paper.

Contents

Introduction: Finding a New Career

Today, changing jobs is an accepted and normal part of life. In fact, according to the Bureau of Labor Statistics, Americans born between 1957 and 1964 held an average of 9.6 jobs from the ages of 18 to 36. The reasons for this are varied: To begin with, people live longer and healthier lives than they did in the past and accordingly have more years of active work life. However, the economy of the twenty-first century is in a state of constant and rapid change, and the workforce of the past does not always meet the needs of the future. Furthermore, fewer and fewer industries provide bonuses such as pensions and retirement health plans, which provide an incentive for staying with the same firm. Other workers experience epiphanies, spiritual growth, or various sorts of personal challenges that lead them to question the paths they have chosen.

Job instability is another prominent factor in the modern workplace. In the last five years, the United States has lost 2.6 *million jobs*; in 2005 alone, 370,000 workers were affected by mass layoffs. Moreover, because of new technology, changing labor markets, ageism, and a host of other factors, many educated, experienced professionals and skilled blue-collar workers have difficulty finding jobs in their former career tracks. Finally—and not just for women—the realities of juggling work and family life, coupled with economic necessity, often force radical revisions of career plans.

No matter how normal or accepted changing careers might be, however, the time of transition can also be a time of anxiety. Faced with the necessity of changing direction in the middle of their journey through life, many find themselves lost. Many career-changers find themselves asking questions such as: Where do I want to go from here? How do I get there? How do I prepare myself for the journey? Thankfully, the Field Guides to Finding a New Career are here to show the way. Using the language and visual style of a travel guide, we show you that reorienting yourself and reapplying your skills and knowledge to a new career is not an uphill slog, but an exciting journey of exploration. No matter whether you are in your twenties or close to retirement age, you can bravely set out to explore new paths and discover new vistas.

Though this series forms an organic whole, each volume is also designed to be a comprehensive, stand-alone, all-in-one guide to getting motivated, getting back on your feet, and getting back to work. We thoroughly discuss common issues such as going back to school, managing your household finances, putting your old skills to work in new situations, and selling yourself to potential employers. Each volume focuses on a broad career field, roughly grouped by Bureau of Labor Statistics' career clusters. Each chapter will focus on a particular career, suggesting new career paths suitable for an individual with that experience and training as well as practical issues involved in seeking and applying for a position.

Many times, the first question career-changers ask is, "Is this new path right for me?" Our self-assessment quiz, coupled with the career compasses at the beginning of each chapter, will help you to match your personal attributes to set you on the right track. Do you possess a storehouse of skilled knowledge? Are you the sort of person who puts others before yourself? Are you methodical and organized? Do you communicate effectively and clearly? Are you good at math? And how do you react to stress? All of these qualities contribute to career success—but they are not equally important in all jobs.

Many career-changers find working for themselves to be more hassle-free and rewarding than working for someone else. However, going at it alone, whether as a self-employed individual or a small-business owner, provides its own special set of challenges. Appendix A, "Going Solo: Starting Your Own Business," is designed to provide answers to many common questions and solutions to everyday problems, from income taxes to accounting to providing health insurance for yourself and your family.

For those who choose to work for someone else, how do you find a job, particularly when you have been out of the labor market for a while? Appendix B, "Outfitting Yourself for Career Success," is designed to answer these questions. It provides not only advice on résumé and self-presentation, but also the latest developments in looking for jobs, such as online resources, headhunters, and placement agencies. Additionally, it recommends how to explain an absence from the workforce to a potential employer.

Changing careers can be stressful, but it can also be a time of exciting personal growth and discovery. We hope that the Field Guides to Finding a New Career not only help you get your bearings in today's employment jungle, but set you on the path to personal fulfillment, happiness, and prosperity.

How to Use This Book

Career Compasses

Each chapter begins with a series of "career compasses" to help you get your bearings and determine if this job is right for you, based on your answers to the self-assessment quiz at the beginning of the book. Does it require a mathematical mindset? Communication skills? Organizational skills? If you're not a "people person," a job requiring you to interact with the public might not be right for you. On the other hand, your organizational skills might be just what are needed in the back office.

Destination

A brief overview, giving you and introduction to the career, briefly explaining what it is, its advantages, why it is so satisfying, its growth potential, and its income potential.

You Are Here

A self-assessment asking you to locate yourself on your journey. Are you working in a related field? Are you working in a field where some skills will transfer? Or are you doing something completely different? In each case, we suggest ways to reapply your skills, gain new ones, and launch yourself on your new career path.

Navigating the Terrain

To help you on your way, we have provided a handy map showing the stages in your journey to a new career. "Navigating the Terrain" will show you the road you need to follow to get where you are going. Since the answers are not the same for everyone and every career, we are sure to show how there are multiple ways to get to the same destination.

Organizing Your Expedition

Fleshing out "Navigating the Terrain," we give explicit directions on how to enter this new career: Decide on a destination, scout the terrain, and decide on a path that is right for you. Of course, the answers are not the same for everyone.

Landmarks

People have different needs at different ages. "Landmarks" presents advice specific to the concerns of each age demographic: early career (twenties), mid-career (thirties to forties), senior employees (fifties) and second-career starters (sixties). We address not only issues such as overcoming age discrimination, but also possible concerns of spouses and families (for instance, paying college tuition with reduced income) and keeping up with new technologies.

Essential Gear

Indispensable tips for career-changers on things such as gearing your résumé to a job in a new field, finding contacts and networking, obtaining further education and training, and how to gain experience in the new field.

Notes from the Field

Sometimes it is useful to consult with those who have gone before for insights and advice. "Notes from the Field" presents interviews with career-changers, presenting motivations and methods that you can identify with.

Further Resources

Finally, we give a list of "expedition outfitters" to provide you with further resources and trade resources.

Make the Most of Your Journey

There are many reasons that you might be contemplating a career change to public service. Jobs working for nonprofit organizations offer intangible benefits although they may not often pay as well as private sector employment. Private companies are motivated by one thing: profit. One way or another, however indirectly, every private sector job is tied to making money for the employer. There is nothing inherently wrong with this arrangement, and the products, services, and innovations provided by the private sector improve everyone's lives substantially. Yet, if you are reading this volume, you may be wondering if there is a more direct way that you could help the less fortunate, support the arts, advocate for a cause you believe in, protect the environment, or put your professional skills to work to make the world a better place. You may be able to find an outlet for these desires with a nonprofit organization. The range of skills needed in this growing employment sector is practically limitless, which means that there is likely to be some nonprofit job that will be a good match for your skills and experience. Each chapter in this volume contains links to Web sites that provide extensive listings for nonprofit vacancies. Once you have read about the required skill set, education, and experience for careers that interest you, you can begin to look for openings in your area.

This volume provides an overview of some of the varieties of public service jobs that are available. Some jobs, such as public official, require that you are elected or appointed to a federal, state, or local government office. Public officials make, execute, enforce, and interpret the laws and policies under which we all live. Your ability to make a transition into a career as a public official will depend on your talents as a public speaker and self-marketer, your capacity to raise campaign funds and spend them judiciously, the support of your family, and, of course, your appeal to voters. If you are angling for an appointed public position, you will have to have the connections and name recognition in your field to secure a nomination. No matter how able a politician you might be, if your policy views are at odds with voters in your town, district, or state, you may be fighting a losing battle. Nonetheless, if you are determined to have a career as an elected official, you will find your public and your niche. Chapter 11 will give you some ideas on how to pursue this exciting career goal.

The transition period for a career change into the public sector varies tremendously by job. Some job transformations can be as quick as picking up the phone and offering your services as a volunteer coordinator for a local museum or charity. Volunteer coordinators recruit, organize, and supervise volunteers in all different types of nonprofit organizations. Volunteers may be used for a few discrete tasks, such as fundraising or ushering, or they may provide all or nearly all of the skilled labor for a nonprofit. The scope of volunteer duties depends on the finances and mission of the organization. Most volunteer coordinators were once volunteers themselves, and they must possess excellent people and organizational skills. Chapter 7 will tell you more about how to turn your passion for a cause into a career as a volunteer coordinator.

Volunteers undertake much of the fundraising work in the nonprofit sector, but each organization usually has an employee who is specifically in charge of raising money for the organization. Unlike in the private sector, where goods or services generate income for the company, nonprofit organizations rely on contributions from altruistic donors to fund their work. Ensuring that a nonprofit organization can continue to perform its public service and pursue its policy goals requires continuous fundraising. The job of fundraiser is certainly not for everyone. You need to have both a passion for the organization's work and a willingness to ask people for money to support it. Chapter 1 talks in more detail about the qualities necessary to pursue a career in fundraising.

A related but distinct occupation to fundraiser is grant administrator. Grant administrators can work for nonprofit organizations that receive funds from the government, private corporations, foundations, or individuals to pursue projects and programs for the public good or advancement of human knowledge and understanding. In this case, the grant administrator is in charge of disbursing grant monies, ensuring that they are used in accordance with the terms of the grant, and reporting back to the funding body on the progress and outcome of the project or program. The job encompasses researching available funding and shepherding the application process, working with researchers and grant writers to present a complete and appealing grant application in time for its deadline. Grant administrators can also work for foundations or government agencies that issue grants. This side of the job requires the administrator to review applications and work with boards and panels that make grant-making decisions. This type of grant administrator must follow up with recipients to track compliance, spending, outcomes, and related administrative matters. The job involves attention to detail and compliance with tax and related laws. You can read more about duties of a grant administrator in Chapter 2.

Recipients of grants can include researchers who work for academic institutions, such as colleges and universities, think tanks, corporations, and other entities that conduct research. Most researchers must possess doctoral degrees, and contribute scholarly articles to their discipline. If you are a practitioner in a scientific or engineering profession and you think you might like to segue into the research end of things, have a look at Chapter 5 to read more about opportunities in this field.

Researchers may stereotypically toil in laboratories and libraries, but some public service jobs involve extensive public interaction and media relations. Publicist and communications manager are two careers that you might consider if you have a background in communications, marketing, advertising, public or media relations, journalism, or writing. Both jobs are related to promoting individuals and organizations and shaping and controlling their public images to portray them in the most favorable light. A publicist usually represents an individual, who can be someone in the entertainment world, such as a musician, actor, writer, or other entertainment star, but publicists also represent politicians and act as spokespeople for government offices. Publicists can also represent nonprofit organizations, such as museums, but people in this role are often called communications directors or managers. Universities, colleges, arts organizations, foundations, and other types of nonprofit institutions often employ communications managers to market their organization to donors and the public. The job entails the equivalent of marketing in a private sector company, so it could be a good fit for someone with a marketing background. See Chapter 10 for more information on a career as a communications manager, and Chapter 4 to learn more about the demanding and busy job of a publicist.

Training is one important job that might not immediately leap off the page at you, but it is worth your consideration, especially if you have a background in education. Like corporate trainers, public trainers teach government and, occasionally, nonprofit employees how to use tools, such as computer software, that are necessary to do their jobs. Some trainers work in-house, as full-time employees of a government agency, and others work on a contract basis as freelance contractors who are sent to various locations as needed. Many trainers today are employed in the technology sector, but other types of training jobs are available. If you think that you might enjoy teaching what you now do, check out Chapter 8 for more detailed information on how to become a trainer.

Another career that you might overlook because it is not as widely publicized is project manager. This line of work is not usually a distinct career track; rather, employees who gain experience and seniority in their job functions may be promoted to leadership positions. Some managers go to school for management degrees and are hired from outside, without moving up from the bottom, and this may be an option for you if you have the requisite schooling. Otherwise, consider how your experience in your industry could be put to use in a management role for a government agency. Civil service jobs may not be as lucrative as some private sector work, but the stability and benefits are legendary. Read more about how to make this stabilizing career transition in Chapter 10.

The final two professions covered in this volume are lobbyist and legal advisor. These jobs are not closely related, but they have some overlap. They both use knowledge as their currency. To lobby government branches effectively for your industry or cause, you must be able to provide accurate information about how a particular piece of legislation will affect your profits or ideological goals. You need to be a master of hard numbers and statistics. A legal advisor must also possess extensive knowledge of how law and policy affect the bottom line or ideological ends of his or her employer. Legal advisors must be lawyers, but lobbyists are often lawyers too. Lobbyists need access to public officials in order to perform their jobs so former public officials are in demand as lobbyists because of their insider knowledge and connections. Lobbyists can also hail from the private sector, representing the interests of an industry or profession in which they have worked. Legal advisors can have virtually any legal background, which makes this field an option for lawyers who have been academics, prosecutors, defense attorneys, corporate associates, or nonprofit lawyers. Peruse Chapter 6 to get a clearer idea of legal advising and take a look at Chapter 3 to learn more about lobbying as a career option. Whatever your reason for entering public service, one of the careers in this volume could be your entrée into this growing employment market.

Self-Assessment Quiz

I: Relevant Knowledge

1. How many years of specialized training have you had?
   - (a) None, it is not required
   - (b) Several weeks to several months of training
   - (c) A year-long course or other preparation
   - (d) Years of preparation in graduate or professional school, or equivalent job experience

2. Would you consider training to obtain certification or other required credentials?
   - (a) No
   - (b) Yes, but only if it is legally mandated
   - (c) Yes, but only if it is the industry standard
   - (d) Yes, if it is helpful (even if not mandatory)

3. In terms of achieving success, how would rate the following qualities in order from least to most important?
   - (a) ability, effort, preparation
   - (b) ability, preparation, effort
   - (c) preparation, ability, effort
   - (d) preparation, effort, ability

4. How would you feel about keeping track of current developments in your field?
   - (a) I prefer a field where very little changes
   - (b) If there were a trade publication, I would like to keep current with that
   - (c) I would be willing to regularly recertify my credentials or learn new systems
   - (d) I would be willing to aggressively keep myself up-to-date in a field that changes constantly

5. For whatever reason, you have to train a bright young successor to do
    your job. How quickly will he or she pick it up?
    (a) Very quickly
    (b) He or she can pick up the necessary skills on the job
    (c) With the necessary training he or she should succeed with
         hard work and concentration
    (d) There is going to be a long breaking-in period—there is
         no substitute for experience

II: Caring

1. How would you react to the following statement: "Other people are the
    most important thing in the world?"
    (a) No! Me first!
    (b) I do not really like other people, but I do make time for them
    (c) Yes, but you have to look out for yourself first
    (d) Yes, to such a degree that I often neglect my own well-being

2. Who of the following is the best role model?
    (a) Ayn Rand
    (b) Napoléon Bonaparte
    (c) Bill Gates
    (d) Florence Nightingale

3. How do you feel about pets?
    (a) I do not like animals at all
    (b) Dogs and cats and such are OK, but not for me
    (c) I have a pet, or I wish I did
    (d) I have several pets, and caring for them occupies significant
         amounts of my time

4. Which of the following sets of professions seems most appealing to
    you?
    (a) business leader, lawyer, entrepreneur
    (b) politician, police officer, athletic coach
    (c) teacher, religious leader, counselor
    (d) nurse, firefighter, paramedic

5. How well would you have to know someone to give them $100 in a harsh but not life-threatening circumstance? It would have to be...
    (a) ...a close family member or friend (brother or sister, best friend)
    (b) ...a more distant friend or relation (second cousin, coworkers)
    (c) ...an acquaintance (a coworker, someone from a community organization or church)
    (d) ...a complete stranger

III: Organizational Skills

1. Do you create sub-folders to further categorize the items in your "Pictures" and "Documents" folders on your computer?
    (a) No
    (b) Yes, but I do not use them consistently
    (c) Yes, and I use them consistently
    (d) Yes, and I also do so with my e-mail and music library

2. How do you keep track of your personal finances?
    (a) I do not, and I am never quite sure how much money is in my checking account
    (b) I do not really, but I always check my online banking to make sure I have money
    (c) I am generally very good about budgeting and keeping track of my expenses, but sometimes I make mistakes
    (d) I do things such as meticulously balance my checkbook, fill out Excel spreadsheets of my monthly expenses, and file my receipts

3. Do you systematically order commonly used items in your kitchen?
    (a) My kitchen is a mess
    (b) I can generally find things when I need them
    (c) A place for everything, and everything in its place
    (d) Yes, I rigorously order my kitchen and do things like alphabetize spices and herbal teas

4. How do you do your laundry?
    (a) I cram it in any old way
    (b) I separate whites and colors

(c) I separate whites and colors, plus whether it gets dried

(d) Not only do I separate whites and colors and drying or non-drying, I organize things by type of clothes or some other system

5. Can you work in clutter?
    (a) Yes, in fact I feel energized by the mess
    (b) A little clutter never hurt anyone
    (c) No, it drives me insane
    (d) Not only does my workspace need to be neat, so does that of everyone around me

IV: Communication Skills

1. Do people ask you to speak up, not mumble, or repeat yourself?
    (a) All the time
    (b) Often
    (c) Sometimes
    (d) Never

2. How do you feel about speaking in public?
    (a) It terrifies me
    (b) I can give a speech or presentation if I have to, but it is awkward
    (c) No problem!
    (d) I frequently give lectures and addresses, and I am very good at it

3. What's the difference between *their, they're,* and *there*?
    (a) I do not know
    (b) I know there is a difference, but I make mistakes in usage
    (c) I know the difference, but I can not articulate it
    (d) *Their* is the third-person possessive, *they're* is a contraction for *they are,* and *there is* a deictic adverb meaning "in that place"

4. Do you avoid writing long letters or e-mails because you are ashamed of your spelling, punctuation, and grammatical mistakes?
    (a) Yes
    (b) Yes, but I am either trying to improve or just do not care what people think

(c) The few mistakes I make are easily overlooked

(d) Save for the occasional typo, I do not ever make mistakes in usage

5. Which choice best characterizes the most challenging book you are willing to read in your spare time?

(a) I do not read

(b) Light fiction reading such as the Harry Potter series, *The Da Vinci Code*, or mass-market paperbacks

(c) Literary fiction or mass-market nonfiction such as history or biography

(d) Long treatises on technical, academic, or scientific subjects

V: Mathematical Skills

1. Do spreadsheets make you nervous?

(a) Yes, and I do not use them at all

(b) I can perform some simple tasks, but I feel that I should leave them to people who arc better-qualified than myself

(c) I feel that I am a better-than-average spreadsheet user

(d) My job requires that I be very proficient with them

2. What is the highest level math class you have ever taken?

(a) I flunked high-school algebra

(b) Trigonometry or pre-calculus

(c) College calculus or statistics

(d) Advanced college mathematics

3. Would you rather make a presentation in words or using numbers and figures?

(a) Definitely in words

(b) In words, but I could throw in some simple figures and statistics if I had to

(c) I could strike a balance between the two

(d) Using numbers as much as possible; they are much more precise

4. Cover the answers below with a sheet of paper, and then solve the following word problem: Mary has been legally able to vote for exactly half her life. Her husband John is three years older than she. Next year,

their son Harvey will be exactly one-quarter of John's age. How old was Mary when Harvey was born?
(a) I couldn't work out the answer
(b) 25
(c) 26
(d) 27

5. Cover the answers below with a sheet of paper, and then solve the following word problem: There are seven children on a school bus. Each child has seven book bags. Each bag has seven big cats in it. Each cat has seven kittens. How many legs are there on the bus?
(a) I couldn't work out the answer
(b) 2,415
(c) 16,821
(d) 10,990

VI: Ability to Manage Stress

1. It is the end of the working day, you have 20 minutes to finish an hour-long job, and you are scheduled to pick up your children. Your supervisor asks you why you are not finished. You:
(a) Have a panic attack
(b) Frantically redouble your efforts
(c) Calmly tell her you need more time, make arrangements to have someone else pick up the kids, and work on the project past closing time
(d) Calmly tell her that you need more time to do it right and that you have to leave, or ask if you can release this flawed version tonight

2. When you are stressed, do you tend to:
(a) Feel helpless, develop tightness in your chest, break out in cold sweats, or have other extreme, debilitating physiological symptoms?
(b) Get irritable and develop a hair-trigger temper, drink too much, obsess over the problem, or exhibit other "normal" signs of stress?
(c) Try to relax, keep your cool, and act as if there is no problem
(d) Take deep, cleansing breaths and actively try to overcome the feelings of stress

3. The last time I was so angry or frazzled that I lost my composure was:
    (a) Last week or more recently
    (b) Last month
    (c) Over a year ago
    (d) So long ago I cannot remember

4. Which of the following describes you?
    (a) Stress is a major disruption in my life, people have spoken to me about my anger management issues, or I am on medication for my anxiety and stress
    (b) I get anxious and stressed out easily
    (c) Sometimes life can be a challenge, but you have to climb that mountain!
    (d) I am generally easygoing

5. What is your ideal vacation?
    (a) I do not take vacations; I feel my work life is too demanding
    (b) I would just like to be alone, with no one bothering me
    (c) I would like to do something not too demanding, like a cruise, with friends and family
    (d) I am an adventurer; I want to do exciting (or even dangerous) things and visit foreign lands

Scoring:

For each category...

For every answer of *a*, add zero points to your score.
For every answer of *b*, add ten points to your score.
For every answer of *c*, add fifteen points to your score.
For every answer of *d*, add twenty points to your score.

The result is your percentage in that category.

Fundraiser

Fundraiser

Career Compasses

Get your bearings on what it takes to be a successful fundraiser.

Caring about the cause for which you are fundraising (20%)

Relevant Knowledge of whom to ask for money and how to approach them (20%)

Ability to Manage Stress is important because it is nerve-wracking to be constantly asking for money and worried about meeting fundraising targets (30%)

Communication Skills are crucial to successful fundraising (30%)

Destination: Fundraiser

The appeal of a career in fundraising is complex. Hardly anyone likes begging people for money, but most of us have a cause dear to our hearts for which we are willing to do so. Opportunities for fundraising come up when, for example, we seek pledges for a charity race, pass the hat for a gift for a colleague, take up a collection for a sick child in our community, or volunteer on a political campaign. A few of us may have been paid for fundraising in college when we worked the phones soliciting funds from alumni. Some of us look on these experiences with dread, cringing with reluctance to ask people for money even when it is for a good cause. If that group includes you, you may want to think about the career of grant administrator (Chapter 2) or another of the many career opportunities in the nonprofit sector. There are some among us who not only do not mind asking for money but also enjoy the challenge and derive a sense of fulfillment from helping a worthy cause gain needed support. If that sounds like you, read on.

Essential Gear

Have a photographic memory. Raising money involves a good deal of massaging the egos of donors. An important key to flattery is recognition. Donors like to feel like VIPs, and being able to remember names and faces will help you make both past and potential contributors feel special. Most types of fundraising involve building relationships with donors whom you will solicit repeatedly for additional contributions. The ability to recall many details about the donor and his or her family and business could make or break a relationship. If you do not have a good memory for names, faces, and personal details, be a prolific note-taker and find excuses to snap photos. Study your notes and photos before your next fundraising event. There are a variety of mnemonics for remembering names—word association games you can play to assist your recollection. Find one that works for you and use it religiously.

Why are you considering a career in fundraising? Is it a natural outgrowth of your current position? You can approach this career from almost any field, but jobs in finance, public relations, marketing, and communications provide one with a particularly relevant background on which to draw. There are no specific degree requirements in fundraising, but a bachelor's—and especially a master's—in public relations, marketing, communications, finance, or even psychology, can prove especially useful. Does fundraising suit your personality? You may not like the actual fundraising part but instead be devoted to the cause for which you are soliciting donations. That is fine, to an extent. Just be aware that fundraising is a draining field that demands total commitment. You will work very long hours for low pay, and much of your work will be done after normal business hours, sometimes at tiresome social functions where you must be "on" like a stage performer. Many if not most donors will turn down your requests for contributions. Do you have a thick enough skin to face repeated rejection and not take it personally? That is an essential trait for a fundraiser. Your salary and bonuses will be much lower than in a for-profit business, but, in addition to the long hours and total commitment already mentioned, your continued employment will be contingent upon meeting your fundraising goals. In the nonprofit universe, you are fundraising to pay your own salary, along with that of every other employee in the organization.

Essential Gear

Pack your best people skills. When you work in sales, you are asking people to give you money in exchange for a good or service. To be a successful salesman, you must convince people that whatever you are selling is worth the price they are paying. A fundraiser has essentially the same job, except that the only thing the purchaser gets in return is the feeling of having done something worthwhile. In some ways that makes your work a little easier, since you are appealing to people's better instincts, but it also poses unique challenges in that you must convince people that your cause is worthwhile and that some concrete good will come from their contribution. In some cases, the donor will be primarily motivated by credit-claiming; in others, givers may wish to remain anonymous. It is your duty to figure out what motivates each potential donor and to tailor your pitch to his or her perspective. This is a crucial skill for success in this field.

The nonprofits that employ fundraisers are many and varied. Some fundraisers, such as those working on political campaigns and for small, locally based charities, are unpaid. If you seek out a volunteer position, that may not qualify as a career change, but with enough available time and dedication, it could certainly feel like one. If you are approaching retirement at your current job but feel like you would like to contribute to the betterment of society, a volunteer fundraising position would provide an ideal opportunity to make use of the time you have to devote to a cause that is meaningful to you. In some nonprofits, fundraising might not be a distinct job function but an endeavor that involves everyone in the organization. This might be a viable option if you have other skills that you could parlay into a position with the nonprofit of your choice. You could contribute your expertise in one area, and learn fundraising on the side. In a large organization, with a more bureaucratic division of labor, you will find that fundraising is a distinct career track, often in a department called "Development." This department will contain various levels of fundraisers, from part-time cold callers to high-level corporate schmoozers, as well as grant writers and grant administrators. In this sort of environment, any management skills that you can carry over from a previous occupation will come in handy. The employees doing the actual grunt work of calling, going door-to-door, or stuffing envelopes may be part-time, temporary, students, or even volunteers, and your job would be to manage them effectively. Whatever the differences in what is done with the money raised, whether it supports a local opera company or is sent overseas to buy textbooks or vaccinations for schoolchildren in the developing world, the process of raising money is similar, and the skill set highly transferable between jobs. Read on for more information on how to find the most appropriate fundraising job for you.

You Are Here

You can begin your journey to fundraising from many different locales.

Do you have connections in the donor community? Most career-level fundraising positions are in an area of development that involves forming lasting relationships with corporations, foundations, various philanthropic entities, and wealthy individuals. If your prior career has given you connections in these worlds, it will be a tremendous advantage. In fact, enough credible name-dropping could be your ticket to your first fundraising job. If you are contemplating this career change, make a list of potential donors that you know well enough to feel comfortable calling.

Have you fundraised in any context? The low pay and high stress of fundraising lead to frequent job turnover, and the lack of specific degree or employment experience requirements make it relatively easy to find a job in fundraising. Most organizations are eager to make room for cadres of unpaid volunteers, but the career ladder in fundraising is tall, and experience can help you start at a higher rung. When you attend a fundraising job interview, your potential employer will want to hear your ideas for fundraising for this particular organization. Enthusiasm and creativity will go a long way, but so will being able to cite statistics on successful fundraising campaigns in your past.

Do you have nonprofit experience? The not-for-profit world can be a scary and unfamiliar place to someone moving from the for-profit sector, or even the public sector in some cases. Budgets are tight and waste is deplored. Whereas the efforts of all employees in a business are firmly fixed on the bottom line, the motivations for the variety of people that fill nonprofit positions are varied and sometimes hard to quantify. If you are used to navigating this universe, it will give you an advantage, even if you have not been previously directly involved in fundraising.

Organizing Your Expedition

Before you set out, know where you are going.

Decide on a destination. What is your passion? Animal rights? Child welfare? The environment? Human rights? Civil rights or civil liberties? Opera? Chamber music? Whatever causes appeal to your sensibilities, there is, without doubt, a nonprofit organization that is raising funds for it right now.

Navigating the Terrain

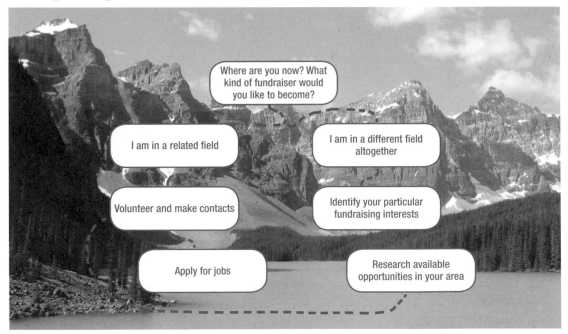

Scout the terrain. One of the first questions any career changer must answer is whether you are willing and able to move. The right job in the career you seek may not be available locally. There are nonprofit organizations raising money in every community in America, and chapters of national charities are widespread, so finding some fundraising position in your local area is likely to be possible wherever you live. The catch is whether the type of position you want is available. If you live far from a major city, you may have a more challenging task finding a position with an arts organization or an international NGO (nongovernmental organization). Do not despair, just make a careful study of where the sorts of jobs that interest you are based and what you have to do to get one of them.

Find the path that's right for you. You could become director of development for a globally recognized NGO, or you could volunteer at an annual fund drive for your favorite local charity, or many options in between. Fundraising is a viable full-time career, and one that is relatively easy to break into, regardless of your previous professional background. It can be an avocation as well as a vocation, an activity you can pursue on a part-time or volunteer basis without leaving your current position. Getting involved with fundraising on a small scale, as a volunteer or for a short-term or recurring campaign, can help you determine if this career is right for you and also provide valuable experience and connections that you can use on the job market. There are also a variety of closely related careers, including grant writer, grant administrator, and, on the other side of the table, director of giving for the philanthropic arm of a business or foundation. With a bit of research and perhaps an internship or two, you will find the position that suits your skills and interests.

Go back to school. There is no specific degree requirement for fundraising, and fundraisers come from a wide variety of educational backgrounds. A degree in the area in which you are fundraising can sometimes be an asset. If you are fundraising for the arts, for example, a degree in art or music can give you an edge as a job applicant, and give you insight into and passion for your cause. The same can be said about the medical field or social services, where a degree in public health or social work does not go amiss. One degree that might be useful is a master's in public administration (MPA), a two-year graduate program that prepares you for a career in public service. Recipients of the MPA degree do not necessarily work for the

Notes from the Field

John Grand
Fundraiser, Planned Parenthood
New York, New York

What were you doing before you decided to change careers?

I was an art history major and throughout college wanted to have a career in museum work; however, rather than focusing on curatorial research, I was more interested in how an institution and its programs interacted with the "outside world." I sent my résumé to the public affairs departments of several museums and ended up getting a position in the development office of one of them. I was paid very little and pushed a lot of paper, but it gave me an incredible "hands-on" introduction to the world of donors and events.

Why did you change your career?

Raising money for arts organizations is wonderful, but I gradually found myself becoming more focused on social service institutions and the impact they have on their communities. A turning point for me was arriving at work on the morning after a big black tie fundraising dinner and having to literally step over two homeless people who were sleeping on the museum's front steps. This was during the mid-1980s when New York City was a very different place. There was a palpable sense of need, and I wanted my work to make more of a difference in

government; most graduates, in fact, use their skills in the service of business or the nonprofit sector. There are several prestigious schools that offer the MPA degree, including Columbia University's School of International and Public Affairs in New York City (http://www.sipa.columbia.edu).

Landmarks

If you are in your twenties . . . You will have no difficulty getting an entry-level fundraising job regardless of your background. Fundraising is a hierarchical career, and the bottom rung of the fundraising career ladder is filled by volunteers, students, and low-paid entry-level workers.

the world around me. I think that we may be facing similar times now, which makes the nonprofit sector especially relevant to social change.

What personal qualities are useful in your profession?

I've always considered myself first and foremost to be a writer, and I think that having strong communication skills, as well as a curious nature, have helped me in my work; however, believing in what you are raising money for is critical, as funders and potential supporters must feel a sense of passion and urgency from you. It also makes the difference between a job that you have passion for and a job that is just a paycheck.

What are the keys to success in your new career?

I've been fortunate to have some really great mentors who have given me wonderful guidance and support. One of the most important things I've been taught is the subtle but crucial difference between "fund-raising" and "development." Fundraising tends to be more of a one-time action—an individual who buys a raffle ticket or comes to an event but never gives again. Development is more about long-term relationship-building—making the effort to understand what motivates a donor, link-ing their interest to your programs, and cultivating them so that their support and commitment grow over time. Having an almost obsessive attention to detail is also essential (nobody likes to see their name spelled wrong, especially in an annual report or newsletter) And, you can never say "thank you" enough.

If you are in your thirties or forties . . . You might want to aim a bit higher in terms of your first fundraising position. The pay of entry-level fundraising positions is often too poor to make it a viable career change option but, if you can convincingly portray your previous job experience as relevant, you might be able to secure a mid-level position with a liv-able salary.

If you are in your fifties . . . Your age and experience are likely to be much more of an asset than a hindrance in this career change. You may have made useful connections in your previous line of work, and you will have had enough social experiences to make you comfortable in a variety of contexts. You have probably learned a considerable amount of tact and patience by the half-century mark, both of which will serve you well in your new field.

If you are over sixty . . . You might consider putting your experience to work for you by becoming a fundraising consultant. A consultant advises less-experienced fundraisers, and nonprofit organizations, on how to raise money, recruit volunteers, obtain donations in kind, or whatever assistance they require. This career would build on related experience that you have accumulated, as well as giving you the opportunity to work with a variety of organizations.

Further Resources

Tony Poderis is an experienced fundraising consultant whose Web site provides advice to neophyte fundraisers. http://www.raise-funds.com

Foundation Center is an organization devoted to raising awareness and knowledge of philanthropy and connecting nonprofits with appropriate resources. http://foundationcenter.org

Independent Sector is a nonprofit coalition of approximately 600 organizations that provides a leadership forum to help charities, foundations, and corporate giving programs pursue their goals effectively to advance the common good. http://www.independentsector.org

Idealist.org is a website that showcases a wide variety of nonprofit organizations and career opportunities available today.

Grant
Administrator

Grant Administrator

Career Compasses

Get your bearings on what it takes to be a successful grant administrator.

Relevant Knowledge of the field in which your grants are used to help you make intelligent grant-making decisions (25%)

Organizational Skills are important in this job as you will be keeping track of a tremendous amount of information (30%)

Mathematical Skills are useful since you are dealing with budgets and financial accounting (20%)

Communication Skills will be of benefit in your dealings with grant recipients (25%)

Destination: Grant Administrator

It should come as no surprise to you that grant administrators administer grants. What you turned to this chapter to find out is what that entails on a day-to-day basis. You want to know if this is a career that might interest you, and if so, what qualifications do you need and how do you make the transition from your current position.

Grant administrators may work for either donor or recipient organizations, although their duties are similar in both types of positions.

12

Grant-making organizations may also be public or private. Public grants come from government agencies, such as the National Science Foundation (NSF). Federal, state, and local governments all give grants, but by far the largest number and dollar amount come from the federal level. The agencies that administer federal grants are generally based in Washington, D.C. There are many potential jobs in this grant-making hub, but you will likely need to live within commuting distance of the capital district to land one.

Essential Gear

Join professional organizations in your new field. There are several professional development membership organizations for grant administrators. Join them and avail yourself of the materials on their Web sites, which may include job listings, and attend their meetings and conferences to network and makes connections in your new field. These will benefit both your initial job search and your subsequent socialization into this line of work.

Private grant-making entities include nonprofits, foundations, and corporate philanthropies. The first type of organization on this list may surprise you. Yes, nonprofits are usually thought of as recipients of grants, but some nonprofits use part of the money they raise to fund projects. At a nonprofit, you could potentially work as a grant administrator on both the donor and recipient sides of the check, depending upon the size of the organization. After the government, the type of grant-making organization that leaps most readily to mind is the foundation. A foundation is also a nonprofit, but it has a permanent funding source of its own, such as a principal fund or endowment. The funds usually come from a single source, such as a corporation, family, or individual who has established a charitable trust. The MacArthur Foundation and the Ford Foundation are two prominent examples. The Bill and Melinda Gates Foundation is now the principal pursuit of the former Microsoft chairman. With an endowment of over $35 billion, it is one of the largest foundations in the world.

A grant administrator working for a recipient organization oversees how received funds are spent and provides support services to program staff, who may be located elsewhere. The grant administrator may work with the organization's legal advisors to draw up all legal documents related to grant-funded projects and create, receive, and analyze financial and progress reports, schedules and project reviews.

The main functions of a grant administrator are to disburse the grant funds, releasing them to individual recipients based on submission of required expense documentation; to maintain and reconcile all financial records related to those funds, including credit card and charge accounts, if used; and—simultaneously—keep the donor happy. Donors will have different expectations regarding progress reports, monitoring, and oversight. Your job is to honor them, hounding the researchers to stick to deadlines and file progress reports in a timely fashion. This aspect of the job requires exceptional communications skills as well as organizational abilities. The job qualifications for a grant administrator in a donor and recipient organization are the same, although knowledge of the scientific, technical or policy field in which the grant is being used is more important in the former role.

Grant-making entities will expect grant administrators to track the submission of all grant applications that are received. The grant administrator will be the contact person for the applicant, and the administrator will inform him or her when additional information is required by the program staffers who are reviewing the proposal. Every donor organization will have some type of database software to keep track of the processing of grant proposals and disbursements. It will be your job to maintain this database, unless you work for a very large organization in which you can delegate routine data processing tasks to subordinates. You will handle all correspondence with grant applicants and recipients, including fielding

Essential Gear

Load your cover letter with related experience. The work of a grant writer has much in common with a variety of other administrative positions. It also shares some similar tasks with accounting and finance-related careers. Even if your previous work seems prima facie unrelated, think about what skills you can draw on and mention those prominently in your résumé and cover letter. If you have any nonprofit experience at all, even in an unrelated position, that can be parleyed to your benefit in your job search as well. Be sure to look carefully at the position requirements and the duties listed in the job description and spell out in your cover letter exactly how your previous work involved using and developing these same skills. Do not make the hiring committee make those connections on their own—they might not see them. Make it easy for them to see how you are the right fit for the position.

queries, drafting award and rejection letters, processing payments, obtaining evaluation and progress reports, and conducting oversight and tracking as called for by each case. You will need to prepare information for your organizations trustees, and possibly attend meetings, acting as a liaison between the trustees and the program staff in your office. There is a lot of filing, both electronic and manual, in this job.

A grant administrator for a recipient organization will also be responsible for overseeing and tracking all grant proposals from members of his or her institution. The administrator is a one-stop shop for proposal writers, such as researchers, to receive information about available grants, keep track of deadlines, and ensure that all pieces of their application are formatted properly and delivered on time. In academic institutions, this is more than a little like herding cats, as professors are notorious for their inability to produce all pieces of an application in advance of a strict deadline. Once a grant is received, the administrator holds the purse strings, keeping careful track of how the funds are spent, following the donor's stipulations as well as all applicable laws and organizational regulations. Grant administrators in universities and nonprofits may be expected to conduct research to find available grants. The continual search for sources of funding may take up as much of your workday as administering funds received. In small organizations, you will be expected to write proposals and make presentations.

In large organizations a grant may fund an entire program, with a large staff of its own. You may function as a human resources manager, overseeing payroll and other personnel management areas. A large, multiyear grant that funds a substantial program may have a grant administrator who is hired to oversee only this specific grant.

The salaries of grant administrators vary widely. A small nonprofit may pay as little as $20,000 per year; however, the average salary for a grant administrator in Washington, D.C., is $81,000. Lower-level grant administrators are little more than glorified clerical workers; higher-level ones may be involved in the decision-making process for issuing grants and may be equipped with a staff. Lower-level vacancies may be open to candidates with only an associate's degree, but higher-level ones may desire an advanced degree. Read on to find out more about how to make the transition into this worthwhile field.

You Are Here

You can begin your journey to becoming a grant administrator from many different locales.

Do you work in fundraising? A grant administrator can be thought of as the flip side of the coin from a fundraiser. A fundraiser solicits money; a grant administrator gives it away. The resemblance ends there, as a fundraiser is not necessarily involved with the administration of the funds he or she obtains, and fundraisers seek contributions from many other types of donors besides grant-making institutions, whereas a grant administrator closely tracks how donated funds are spent. Nonetheless, previous work as a fundraiser would afford you valuable experience in the nonprofit world, a sense of the financial needs and budgets of nonprofit organizations, as well as connections with donors that may prove useful when you are searching for your first grant-administrator position.

Do you have a degree or experience in the field in which you will administer grants? Grant administrators use a variety of criteria to evaluate the merits of applications and some elements of a good application transcend disciplines. Yet a research project or program that appears worthy may have flaws in its basic hypothesis, research design, usefulness, or appropriateness that may not be apparent to someone without specialized knowledge of the field in question. It might, for example, duplicate previous research or contain methodological errors that would affect the accuracy and usefulness of the results. If you have an educational or career-related background in any of the sciences, or in a particular policy area, play this up in your job applications.

Do you have a background in grant writing? It is difficult to imagine a more appropriate background for a grant administrator than having been a grant writer in a previous life. Grant writing is a distinct skill and a successful grant writer has intimate knowledge of what makes an application stand out, and is familiar with all the tricks of the trade to give the donor what they want to hear. You cannot fool a former grant writer; they can smell insincerity wafting off the page. For this reason alone, donors are always eager to hire former grant writers to administer their grants.

Navigating the Terrain

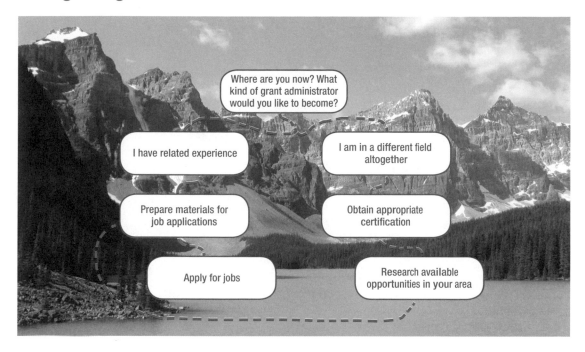

Where are you now? What kind of grant administrator would you like to become?

I have related experience

I am in a different field altogether

Prepare materials for job applications

Obtain appropriate certification

Apply for jobs

Research available opportunities in your area

Organizing Your Expedition

Before you set out, know where you are going.

Decide on a destination. First, you will need to decide if you want to work for a donor or recipient organization. Within either of those broad categories, you will have further choices to make. On the donor side, you could work for a foundation, the philanthropic department of a corporation, or a government entity. With the public sector, there are three levels of government from which to choose—local, state, or federal—and within the federal government there are myriad grant-making agencies. On the recipient side, you could work for a university, research institute, corporation, or nonprofit. Some organizations can be both donors and recipients of grant funds; such as universities, which may give grants to their own faculty members; and nonprofits, which can issue project grants to further their mission. The working atmosphere in academia, government, and the for-profit and nonprofit sectors can be quite different, and much

Notes from the Field

Jane Hargreaves
Research administrator
Amherst, Massachusetts

What were you doing before you decided to change careers?

I was working as a proposal writer for a pubic health nonprofit. I have an MSW (master's in social work) and my career took me into the area of grant writing over a period of about 10 years.

Why did you change your career?

My husband obtained a professorship at University of Massachusetts, and we moved to the Amherst area. I was looking for a job, and this seemed like a good fit with my background.

How did you make the transition?

I'm afraid I don't have a dramatic story to tell: I applied and I was offered the job. Initially I thought about looking for something part-time

about it depends on the size and wealth of the organization. Consider the environment in which you feel most at home.

Scout the terrain. Speaking of home, assess what jobs are available where you live now, and whether and where you are willing to move for a grant-administrating job. If you live near a major research university, that is a logical place to begin your search. If you hail from a state capital, look into jobs with state agencies. Foundations and federal government agencies tend to be concentrated in the District of Columbia, but there are foundations in most major cities. Search online job postings to get an idea what positions are being advertised in your locale. If the right job is not available within commuting distance, consider whether you are willing to move to pursue this career change. If you have a family, consult with them about their feelings on the issue.

Find the path that's right for you. There are many ways of putting money to good use in the world. Whether you help wealthy donor organizations choose worthy recipients for their funds or link laudable *or working as a freelance proposal writer, but the cost of living here is really too high for that to be a viable option.*

What are the keys to success in your new career?

Being well-organized is a nice trait to possess if you want to keep your sanity. There is a lot of information to keep track of; this is a paperwork-intensive job. If you aren't organized, you will miss deadlines or misplace components of an application. One aspect of the job that surprised me a little, coming from proposal writing, is how much you need to know about taxes. I thought accountants or legal advisors took care of much of that, but, no, it's the administrators who must be familiar with it and make sure every dollar is accounted for in the proper way, and that the right forms go out to the right people—on time!

researchers and commendable nonprofits with the funding they need to operate, you will have the satisfaction of knowing your professional efforts are worthwhile. If you have experience writing proposals, you might lean toward working for a university or other organization where you could help researchers put together the best possible applications. On the other hand, you might relish the philanthropy side of being the one giving out the money instead of the one asking for it.

Go back to school. There are usually no specific degree requirements for grant administrators, although in most instances it is safe to say that you would never get an interview without at least a bachelor's degree. It can be helpful to have a degree in finance, human resources, or management. Also useful is a degree in a field in which research grants are commonly given, which includes most of the sciences. Professional development organizations such as the National Grants Management Association (NGMA) and the National Association of College and University Business Officers (NACUBO), as well as the membership organizations listed in Further Resources, offer continuing education courses, training course, and seminars that lead to various forms of certification. It is wise to investigate what certification is needed for the job that you want. Community affairs divisions of state government offer weekend training for between $100 and $200 to administrators wishing to certify to manage public block grants. Some states offer a test-out option where aspirants pay a fraction to demonstrate the proficiency of their knowledge. Especially in an era when states and nongovernmental organizations are looking to patch holes in their budgets or falloffs in donations from their bases, the role of the grant administrator in securing precious funds is more crucial than ever. Those who occupy this important position will be expected to attend continuing-education courses on a regular basis to keep up to speed in this dynamic field.

Landmarks

If you are in your twenties . . . You probably do not yet have a lot of transferable skills, but do not let that worry you. If you have some office experience, nonprofit experience, or a finance or human resources degree, you should be able to get an entry-level job or even a mid-level job in some organizations.

If you are in your thirties or forties . . . You are likely to have a related position or transferable skill set if you are contemplating a move to grant administrating. Use what professional connections you have made to help you make the transition. If you are moving from a significantly different field, take a certification course to bolster your credentials.

If you are in your fifties . . . The advice given about for career changers in their thirties or forties still applies to you: market your transferable skills and work your connections, take a certification course to show potential employers that you are knowledgeable and serious about this career path.

If you are over sixty . . . You should know that grant administrators work long hours at the office doing detailed and often tedious computer work. This is not a position to consider if you want a second, less-taxing career in retirement. But if you have the interest and the energy, you are likely to face a welcoming workplace where your experience will be valued.

Further Resources

National Council of University Research Administrators (NCURA) is the leading professional development organization for research administrators, another name for grant administrators, who work in universities. http://www.ncura.edu

Society of Research Administrators (SRA) International is one of the main professional organizations for research administrators. It has approximately 4,000 members, who work for the federal government, and at universities, nonprofits and hospitals. http://www.srainternational.org/sra03/index.cfm

Proposal Writer.com is a useful resource for grant writers. It contains detailed information on how to respond to an RFP (Request for Proposals). http://www.proposalwriter.com

Foundation Center is a one-stop shop with oodles of information for both grant makers and grant seekers. http://foundationcenter.org

Lobbyist

Lobbyist

Career Compasses

Get your bearings on what it takes to be a successful lobbyist.

Relevant Knowledge of your issue area is essential to do your job effectively (40%)

Organizational Skills to keep track of names, dates, legislation, finances, etc. (20%)

Communication Skills are the key to success in your job (30%)

Ability to Manage Stress is useful because your job is always on the line (10%)

Destination: Lobbyist

Lobbyists frequently get a bad rap. One often reads or hears cynical descriptions of public policy claiming that it was written by lobbyists or that elected officials have bought their offices by accepting the contributions of lobbyists, putting them in the pockets of the lobbyists and their policy agenda. Sometimes elected officials get caught accepting illegal gifts from lobbyists and are excoriated for earlier images golfing or

23

hunting with them. Lobbyists also do their most effective work outside the public eye, leaving little to challenge the pervasive negative view of them as private influence peddlers whose clients' interests often conflict with the public good. Clearly, this perception has considerable basis in fact. Corporate lobbyists are working to advance the policy agenda of their particular industry; unlike elected officials, they have no obligation to serve the public interest, and they can be willfully myopic. But this chapter will demonstrate that there is more to lobbying than promoting private business interests. Many lobbyists work for nonprofits, which assert that they are working for the public interest rather than personal economic gain.

Essential Gear

Be a joiner. From the local to the national level, there are a multitude of political, religious, civic, charitable, and other organizations that you can join. Become a member of as many as possible, and work your way up the ranks, volunteering or running for officer positions. This is not the time to appear evenhanded or nonpartisan. Pick a side and stick to it. Your credibility will be greater if you do.

Of course, what is in the public interest is a matter of opinion. A pro-choice organization that is working to liberalize abortion rights and access firmly believes that it is working in the public interest. Yet, an anti-choice organization that is lobbying equally hard to restrict abortion rights and access is also absolutely convinced that it is acting for the public welfare, as do the contributors and supporters of each of these diametrically opposed so-called public interest groups. One thing is common to all public interest groups: They are nonprofit organizations that do not derive financial gain from the activities linked to their policy preferences. The coal industry makes money from mining coal and the policies it promotes have only one objective: increasing its profits. Thus, the motivation and objectives of nonprofit lobbyists are more complex. They believe there is some value in the public policies they promote, but they are not going to line their pockets by getting them passed.

There is one other category of lobbyists, besides business and nonprofit, that we should mention at least briefly: the government lobbies themselves. Local government lobbies the state for funds and policies favorable to its economic, social, and civic interests. State governments lobby the federal government for the exact same things, and bureaucratic agencies within the federal government, such as the Environmental Protection Agency (EPA), Department of Transportation (DOT), Department of Health and Human Services (DHHS), Department of Defense (DOD), Department of Interior (DOI), Department of Energy (DOE), and all other government agencies beyond these few examples lobby for increased funding and legislation that will augment the power and prestige of their agency.

Now that you are acquainted with three categories of lobbyists, you might be interested to learn more about how lobbyists in all sectors do their jobs. It is clear *what lobbyists do*: they "lobby," that is, petition the government for legislation that benefits their clients in a monetary or ideological fashion. To whom within government do they appeal? Usually the legislative branch: At the local level, this may be a city council or county board. At the state level, they would focus on the members of the state legislature. Congress, of course, would be their target at the national level. Lobbyists do not focus all of their resources on legislatures. The executive has considerable power regarding the passage and shaping of public policy. The executive usually has to sign a bill passed by the legislature in order for it to become law. He or she can help set the policy agenda, influencing which bills are acted on by the legislature, as well as exerting the office's considerable leverage to shape the substance of the policy and put a spin on it for the public.

Also, let us not forget implementation. Executive agencies take on a policymaking role when they implement legislation. A law is only as good as its funding and enforcement. Often legislation passed by Congress or other legislatures is vague and much of its effectiveness

The seasoned lobbyist knows many tactics.

is determined by how rules are defined and implemented by the relevant agencies. A lobbyist who is unsuccessful in stopping passage of a piece of legislation that his or her client opposes can still weaken its impact considerably by lobbying the agency charged with implementing it.

The judicial branch also plays a role in policymaking. Judges interpret laws, which determines what those vaguely written laws actually mean in practice. The fact that many lobbyists are lawyers increases their affinity for the judicial side of lawmaking; nonetheless, the reactive role of the judicial system makes it harder to lobby effectively. The Supreme Court cannot hold a press conference and declare, "This is what law X means." Instead, they must wait until a case lands on their docket to interpret statutes. Lobbyists can wine and dine judges in an effort to influence how they will rule in certain types of cases, and they can contribute to judicial campaigns for state and local judicial elections. They can also file amicus curiae (friend of the court) briefs in specific cases. As interest groups increasingly turn to the courts rather than legislatures to advance their policy goals, lobbying of judges may increase.

Lobbying can be a lucrative and exciting career, but the pay scale depends upon your industry. Corporate lobbyists can expect seven-figure salaries, but lobbyists at small nonprofits are looking more in the low five-figure range. The ability of an organization to lobby multiple levels of government—local, state, and federal—and to maintain a permanent office and staff in a state or national capital is dependent upon its size and financing. Most lobbyists expect to be paid well for their services, and to have a sizable budget for entertaining officials. Access to many perks goes with the territory, but so does risk. Successful lobbyists can make a fortune, but unsuccessful ones do not last long.

Career changers have an advantage in entering the lobbying field in that it is generally a line of work you must enter from another field because a person with no job experience is unlikely to have the industry or issue knowledge required for effective lobbying. Read on for more information on transforming your knowledge and connections into a viable, profitable career as a lobbyist.

You Are Here

You can begin your journey to lobbying from many different locales.

Do you have political connections? This question is first for a reason: The currency of lobbyists is connections, because they bring access to legislators and other government officials who are in a position to influence policy. Without a strong network of political connections, you are unlikely to make a successful career transition into the world of lobbying. Your résumé in this field is the people you know. If you have connections via your job, your hobbies, your family, or your civic engagement, any will help get your foot in the door.

Do you know your industry or issue area well? Studies have shown that effective lobbying is related to more than just who has the best box seats or ability to get reservations at the most exclusive restaurants or even who can raise the most campaign donations. Research grounds the profession. The most crucial bargaining chip that a lobbyist brings to the table is *knowledge*. Lobbyists need to know the ramifications of each bill for their industry and its effects on things the official in question cares about.

Some lobbyists are motivated by a desire to serve a cause.

Do you have stellar research skills? You will need them to find out every possible bill that might affect your issue or industry, to learn which officials should be your lobbying targets for a given bill, and what tools from your lobbying toolbox to employ with each of them. One may bristle at an approach that is too forward and throw you out of his or her office—but be open to arguments, backed up with carefully researched statistics, of how a proposed bill might hurt his or her constituents. Another may care less about the effects of a bill than about your willingness to make a hefty contribution to a charity run by his or her spouse. Lobbying is not one-size-fits-all. Although money talks, so do facts and figures, and you need to know how to work them both, and to wield them in discussion with élan.

Organizing Your Expedition

Before you set out, know where you are going.

Decide on a destination. As you have seen, there are three main bases from which you can lobby—the business sector, the nonprofit sector, and the government itself. Business lobbying is by far the most lucrative, but money may not be your only consideration. You may be motivated to lobby for a cause dear to your heart, or you may want to lobby for your current industry or profession. There are links provided at the end of this chapter for several Web sites with job listings for potential lobbyists. Looking at these advertisements can help you get a feel for what qualifications and experience are being sought in different sectors. Your final lobbying destination is going to be closely linked to the career you have

Stories from the Field

Liz Robbins
Liz Robbins & Associates, Inc.
New York and Washington, D.C.

Throughout former president Bush's first term in office, he was dogged by the accusation that his vice president, Dick Cheney, and other members of his cabinet were the real decision-makers behind the scenes. This idea that there are powerful people in Washington, D.C., that escape media attention and celebrity status is personified in lobbyist Liz Robbins. Robbins has made a 32 year (so far) career out of lobbying politicians in Washington on behalf of causes she believes in, not on behalf of big business. Both her longevity in the business and her dedication to cause lobbying are remarkable. Although she cannot afford to be partisan in her line of work, she is widely considered a Democratic lobbyist and she is a "Friend of Bill." Hillary attended her wedding, to television journalist Doug Johnson. Although Robbins may be the bigshot Washington power player in that couple, you would never recognize her on the street, whereas her husband's face and voice are familiar to millions of Americans from his years as a television reporter on ABC. But members of the legislative and executive branches would recognize Robbins, since she has made it her job to be known and liked by them. In a still very much male-dominated field, Robbins founded the first female-headed lobbying firm in Washington.

Liz Robbins grew up in Westchester, New York, and majored in philosophy at Wheaton College in Massachusetts. She initially pursued an advertising career in New York, but a Congressional internship solidified her nascent desire to enter public service. After working for a few Senate committees, she obtained her first lobbying gigs working for state

had so far because your ability to get a job is going to be based on the knowledge you possess and the connections you have made.

Scout the terrain. Most job searches are constrained by the applicant's willingness and ability to move to where the jobs are. Aspiring lobbyists should know their thoughts about moving for a better prospect and should be aware that the job itself usually involves lots of travel. Most and local governments that were suffering financial exigency. New York, Michigan, and San Francisco were some of her first clients. Over time, she developed certain areas of issue specialization, including taxes, intellectual property, and foster-care legislation, with education issues as her central focus due to her stint working for the Department of Education. Her work in this issue area primarily consists of bringing federal dollars to worthy educational programs at the state and local level and making federal education programs more responsive to local needs. She maintains a mix of clients that enables her to pursue lobbying efforts on behalf of nonprofit organizations with limited lobbying budgets. Her firm does not take clients unless she personally supports their cause.

Many people think of "lobbyist" as a dirty word and the lobbying of members of Congress and other government officials with the purpose of influencing decision-making, legislation or appropriations to be sleazy, reprehensible behavior. Under some circumstances, it can be, such as when a polluting industry buys votes against environmental regulations. But the career of Liz Robbins demonstrates that lobbyists can achieve influence and success by going to bat for well-meaning nonprofit organizations that are striving to get support from the government. Petitioning the government on behalf of policies that concern you is the right of all citizens, but most of us do so in sporadic informal ways instead of doing it for a living. When you write to your local school board asking them not to cut an arts program that benefits your children, you are essentially doing what Liz Robbins does on a smaller scale. To a large extent, her work involves persuading elected officials to take an interest in certain issues that would otherwise not receive federal attention and dollars. In a certain sense, it is not too far removed from her youthful work in advertising, although it is likely to be more gratifying.

lobbying arms of businesses, nonprofits, and government agencies are located in and around Washington, D.C. For groups that focus their lobbying efforts at the state level, residence in or near your state capital will be required.

Find the path that's right for you. The fact that you are reading this chapter means that something is drawing you to a career shift into lob-

Navigating the Terrain

bying. It may be money; it may be a quest for power and influence, or it may be a strong commitment to a cause or profession. Whatever your motivation, you should be able to match it with an appropriate lobbying job. Carefully consider and inventory your areas of experience and expertise as they relate to policy, and weigh where you would see your research aptitudes and connections making the best combination.

Another tip for making the transition is to remember that the people with the most inside access to elected officials are usually former elected officials. Former legislators are always in demand as lobbyists and many people run for public office specifically to lay the groundwork for a future lobbying career. So, your path to a lobbying job may take you first along a detour of public service. Running for public office is a career-changing venture in itself (and it is the subject of Chapter 11).

Go back to school. There is no such thing as a degree in lobbying, but several degrees can prove useful, most notably public relations and marketing. After all, you are engaged in marketing your client to legislators and other public servants. As noted previously, many lobbyists are lawyers, so a law degree is a tremendous asset. There is some value in attending school aside from the degree that you pursue, as university can afford opportunities to join political organizations, obtain internships, and begin the crucial process of making political connections.

Landmarks

If you are in your twenties . . . This is the time to begin making political connections. If you are in college or graduate school, join the campus Republicans or Democrats and volunteer for political campaigns. Join some charitable organizations or try your hand at founding your own educational or independent 527 nonprofit for your cause of choice to learn the ropes of fundraising and lobbying. Pick a first career—like law, for the general training; or engineering, for providing a basis of understanding capital-rich industries—that will help you segue into lobbying later.

If you are in your thirties or forties . . . You are old enough to begin to run for officer and board positions in your organizations, or even to run for pubic office. Remember that many lobbyists are former elected officials; any experience of group leadership may be helpful, and organizations are a tried-and-true method. This is also the ideal time to make the career transition to lobbying. Depending upon your current job, you might be able to move into lobbying for your current employer or industry, especially if you work for a large corporate law firm.

Essential Gear

Make friends along the way. Lobbyists spend their days (and sometimes their nights) trying to get legislators and other government officials to give them an audience. The higher up an official, the more useful she or he is to a lobbyist, and the more difficult to buttonhole due to the many demands on their time. The key to getting the official ear is to become a personal friend of the family. This way you are not roadblocked by secretaries when you try to make an office appointment; rather, you can chat over beers at a family barbeque on the weekend. If you cannot initially gain access to the official herself or himself, work on making family connections. Think of strategies like signing your son up to play on the same soccer team as your target's son or having your spouse join the same charity board as your target's spouse. Welcome to life as a lobbyist!

If you are in your fifties . . . It is time to make your move, if you have not yet done so, and go all out for your lobbying dream job. You should have all of your ducks in a row, in terms of political connections, by now. If you do not, it is a bit late to start, but perhaps doable if you are energetic and highly motivated. Business connections are also a political resource, if they are a little special and you handle them right.

If you are over sixty . . . As noted above, if you have not yet begun to prepare the groundwork for a transition into lobbying, it is a bit late to start. You are hooked in, or you are not so hooked in—and you probably know. But even if you lack political connections, you might be able to parley your knowledge and experience in your current field into a lobbying job on behalf of your employer or industry. Other satisfying policy-related jobs discussed in this volume include grant administrator (Chapter 2), which can valuably apply a long perspective on a particular field.

Further Resources

The Ladders is a job search Web site that features jobs paying over $100K. This includes many private sector lobbying positions. http://www.theladders.com

Get Lobbyist Jobs is, as you might expect, a resource for lobbying jobs. It has nationwide job listing for all types of lobbyist positions in the public, private and nonprofit sectors. http://www.getlobbyistjobs.com

Lobbying Jobs.com is another comprehensive source of lobbyist job listings. http://www.lobbyingjobs.com

The Lobbyist Program provides information about how to get a lobbyist job and what to do once you have it. Site made by the Montana YMCA Youth and Government program. http://home.mcn.net/~montanabw/lobbyist.html

Publicist

Publicist

Career Compasses

Get your bearings on what it takes to be a successful publicist.

Relevant Knowledge of promotion tactics and strategies (25%)

Organizational Skills to keep track of your media contacts and clients (25%)

Ability to Manage Stress is helpful because book launches, premieres, and other events will place you under a great deal of pressure. (20%)

Communication Skills are key to performing this job effectively (30%)

Destination: Publicist

So, you are interested in a career in sales. You are in the right place; a publicist is a salesperson: You are selling your client. Many of the same qualities that make a good salesperson are needed to be a successful publicist. You must be "a people person:" That is, you must like meeting people, talking to them, and you must be able to make quick, accurate judgments. It also helps—no point in mincing words here—if you are a bit pushy and not willing to take "no" for an answer. There is an important caveat, however: In order to promote his or her client, a publicist uses contacts in various media. If you are too aggressive or pushy, you might alienate important contacts, so good judgment about exactly how far to push your contacts is essential.

Good judgment also comes in handy in deciding where and how to promote your client. There is a saying that there is no such thing as bad publicity, but, in truth, some publicity stunts can backfire if they are considered tasteless or target an inappropriate audience or use an inappropriate medium for your client. The days of merely getting your client's name mentioned in the papers are long over. Today's consumers are inundated with information, including massive amounts of advertising, both direct and indirect. Most people learn to filter and tune out information that they do not consider relevant to themselves. The proliferation of media outlets may make your job easier in some respects, but, on the whole, it makes it more challenging because it is harder to stand out from the cacophony of information noise in various media. A good publicist knows how to target the right media for his or her client.

Keeping your client's name *out of the news* is also part of the job. Damage control has always been part of a publicist's job description, but today, with camera phones and microphones always at the ready to record gaffes both major and minor, unflattering publicity is a constant rather than intermittent problem. In fact, you can count on diffusing bad publicity to encompass at least half of your time, and even most of it with certain types of clients.

A publicist's job managing a client's image has become so comprehensive today that many publicists have staff and managing the staff is another necessary skill. Publicists may organize large events, which

Essential Gear

Search the horizon for an internship. Would you hire a publicist with no experience? There is a general reluctance to spend money on an employee that may or may not be able to do the job, and who will spend a fair amount of the company's time and money just learning the ropes. The way around this is via an internship. If you can afford to work for free, at least temporarily, you can acquire the necessary experience to land your first PR gig. In fact, employers tend to look to their own interns first to fill open positions. Do not let age or previous experience in another field be a barrier; an internship could be your ticket to a new career as a publicist.

require tremendous coordination and organizational skills, as well as a good memory for names and sense of protocol. Publicists today may be called upon to give multimedia presentations, so technical acumen (or a good tech staff), public speaking ability, and a sense of visual design as well as a way with words are all part of the skills package of the modern publicist.

That may seem like a daunting array of talents and skills for one career path. For whom do publicists make such a multifaceted effort? Actors and musicians probably leap to mind first, as well as writers, politicians, and perhaps other television personalities, like celebrity chefs, dog trainers, designers, and, perhaps, pundits. But many organizations need publicists, including museums, charities, schools at all levels, hospitals, and even Web sites—not to mention corporations and other businesses in every industry under the sun. Not all of these jobs are equally lucrative or high-profile; a publicist for a children's charity is not going to make the same kind of salary or travel in the same circles as a publicist for a singer with number one hit records or an Academy Awarding-winning actor. Publicists earn around $50,000 at the lower end, although neophyte publicists may make less. Publicists for large corporate clients can expect to earn in the neighborhood of $200,000, and, of course, celebrity publicists can make millions, although, just as with celebrities themselves, there are many more wannabes than there are million-dollar publicists.

By the same token, though all publicists try to obtain good publicity for their clients and limit the dissemination of bad publicity, the exact needs of each type of client will vary. A hospital, a car company, an

Essential Gear

Put up a Web site. Traditional media outlets are still the mainstay of the PR world, but the Internet is a growing area in this field. If you have Web design skills, put up a Web site that showcases your credentials. If you can, volunteer to put up a promotional Web site for an up-and-coming artist or a local organization. A restaurant is a great choice for this type of promotional practice. Think of creative ways to promote them, such as photographing celebrities dining there. This free work will become a valuable part of your portfolio, so think of it as building your skills and credentials. Write some press releases and work your press contacts to get them in the local papers and on local television and radio. Then parlay this experience into your first paying job in your new field.

elected official, and a writer need somewhat different services from a publicist and will look for slightly different specialty areas of skills and experience when hiring one.

The background of publicists with different types of clientele can vary considerably. Certain degrees and work experience are more appropriate than others. A background in or degree in advertising may leap to mind as the obvious choice, but in truth, as a publicist, you are less designing an advertising campaign than selling the existing one. This limits the direct correlation to an advertising background, but it is still a previous line of work or prior degree that could open some doors as you try to make your career change. Likewise, courses or experience in marketing are useful, but not precisely aligned with what you will do as a publicist. The ideal degree is public relations (PR), or media relations as some schools are calling it. Of course, if you already had experience in PR, you would not be changing careers, but it is not unusual for job applicants to have a degree or to have taken individual courses in a subject area in which they have not worked. This is the time to play those up if you have them. Second best to PR would be a degree or experience in journalism. The "why" here should be pretty straightforward: As a publicist, you will be trying to get information into the press and keep other information out of it and control the "spin" or slant of any mention of your clients. You will be writing a lot of press releases and dealing with reporters on a daily basis. A background in journalism would be a golden ticket to your new career in PR. Read on for more information on how to make the leap into the exciting world of public relations.

You Are Here

You can begin your journey to becoming a publicist from many different locales.

Could you promote the field in which you now work? If you split the job of publicist into two required areas of knowledge, knowledge of *what you are promoting* (singer, winery, president) and *how to promote* (writing ability, confidence, credibility, press connections), you are going to need to start off with at least one of these on your résumé. Consider your current employer: Does your company have a PR department? Do they hire outside publicists as consultants or contractors? If they have an internal PR department, talk to your human resources department about segueing into it. If they hire outside consultants, investigate the possibility of quitting your current job and being rehired as an independent contractor.

Do you have any media experience? At the opposite end of the spectrum from knowing the industry that you are promoting is knowing the press. In fact, media experience is widely considered more valuable than experience in the business you are promoting. If you have journalism experience, whether for a newspaper, Web site, television or radio, that fact should be the centerpiece of your résumé and cover letter. This is not the time to be shy about name-dropping. Make a list of every media outlet for which you have worked, and everyone you know who is in a position to get a press mention for a potential client. Even if you just shook hands with them at a party, if you would feel comfortable calling them, put down their name. Remember that your first PR client is yourself. Your ability to sell yourself is the ticket to your first publicist position.

Have you promoted anything or anyone? You may not have worked formally in public relations but you have probably promoted something. Consider not only your paid professional background but also any volunteer experience you have had. Did you organize a local 5K run for charity? Do you put on the local Christmas pageant in your community? Do you help organize the annual fundraiser for your child's basketball team? Experiences like these can be played up on a résumé to show your motivation and talents in the area of promotions.

Organizing Your Expedition

Before you set out, know where you are going.

Decide on a destination. Publicists work in many different industries so your first decision is going to involve asking yourself what you would like to promote. If you have experience in one field, you may be inclined to promote it based on your inside knowledge of that industry. If you have worked in the wine industry, for example, you may find the idea

Navigating the Terrain

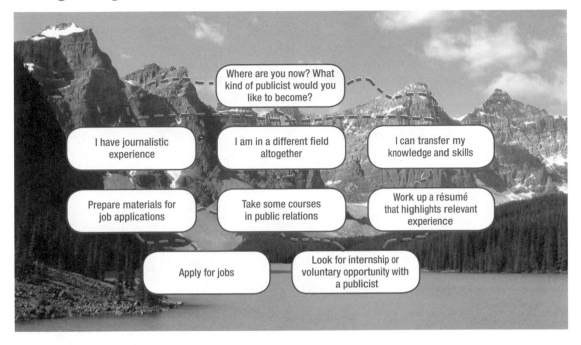

Where are you now? What kind of publicist would you like to become?

I have journalistic experience

I am in a different field altogether

I can transfer my knowledge and skills

Prepare materials for job applications

Take some courses in public relations

Work up a résumé that highlights relevant experience

Apply for jobs

Look for internship or voluntary opportunity with a publicist

of becoming a publicist for a vineyard appealing. Your experience and connections in the wine business would be an asset in acquiring clients. If your current field is not one that uses publicists extensively, or if you want to make a move to an entirely different industry, then you have plenty of options. Virtually every industry in the private sector uses publicists, and the nonprofit sector increases your choices considerably. Is there an industry that interests you? Sports promotion is a popular choice, as is the energy industry. Is there a cause that you believe in strongly? If animal rights or finding a cure for pediatric cancer move you, that might be an area in which to investigate jobs. One of the biggest PR markets is the public sector. The most visible publicist in the United States is the president's press secretary. That job is unlikely to be open to someone without considerable prior experience, but there are plenty of other publicists employed by governments at all levels.

Scout the terrain. Most industries are geographically concentrated, and PR is no exception. PR jobs tend to be concentrated in major media,

Notes from the Field

Michael Busack
Publicist, Historic Deerfield
Deerfield, Massachusetts

What were you doing before you decided to change careers?

First and foremost I have always been a writer. I think my passion for writing and politics easily led me to an interest and eventual love for journalism. A great justice can be done for the general public with honest and accurate reporting. I was intrigued by the ability to play watchdog to government and provide a service to the public.

Why did you change your career?

When I received my first full-time reporting position at a respected newspaper, I thought, "Wow, this is really going to be my opportunity to do something important." After about a year, however, I realized that due to the convergence of media into many new Web-based formats, journalism is transitioning into an entirely different animal. I wasn't happy with the quality and voice of the assignments I was being given. I realized that this job was a reflection of the industry. I also understood

political, and arts and entertainment markets such as New York, Washington, D.C., Los Angeles, San Francisco, and Chicago. The advent of the Internet has increased job opportunities in other cities so, do not despair if you do not live in one of these places. Start by looking for listings for PR firms in your city. Look at their Web sites and ask to schedule an informational interview with them to find out what sort of PR they do and what skills, experience, and coursework you need to get a job. All but the largest PR firms are likely to concentrate on certain industries, and even further specialize within that sector, such as a music PR firm specializing in rap artists. In addition to PR firms, research what industries are prominent in your locality. Who has corporate headquarters there? What sort of museums do you have? What large charities are based there? And do not forget the world of politics: Do you live in or near your state capital or a major city in your state? The office of the mayor may employ publicists, and governors certainly do.

that I have a wide variety of interests and talents, and I liked the challenge of applying them in a new format.

How did you make the transition?

When I decided to delve into publicity, I knew that I had to be wary of burning bridges. Since a reporter and publicist are separated by objectivity, I wanted to be careful to search for jobs that would not disqualify my candidacy for future positions that may demand objectivity. I found that I could use my love of history and art, and my talent and understanding of the media, as a publicist for Historic Deerfield, an open-air history and art museum in Deerfield, Massachusetts. This was a decision that had a very low risk of future conflicts.

What are the keys to success in your new career?

I think a mantra for a publicist should be "know your customer." When I am trying to spread the word about our organization, I am constantly seeking to get the right message to the right people. This takes time, research, an ability to write effectively, and a knack to build and secure relationships with the right people. If you think you have those characteristics, then a career in publicity might just be for you.

Find the path that's right for you. This is the point at which you need to be completely honest with yourself. You need a tremendous amount of enthusiasm and energy to be an effective publicist, and that will be easier to muster if it reflects your genuine sentiments about your client. In political PR, partisanship will determine your career options, as a Republican would never be hired to work for a Democrat and vice versa. In the arts, likewise follow your passion. Do you love classical music? Opera? Jazz? Your knowledge and enthusiasm will impress potential employers and help compensate for a lack of concrete experience in your new field.

Go back to school. There are no specific degree requirements for publicists, but a degree in public relations or media relations is ideal. A journalism or communications degree is a close second. Advertising and marketing would be your third choices. Individual courses are nearly as useful as a degree in any of these fields. If you are not willing or able to return to school for a degree but you have discovered that you need to bolster your résumé to land your first PR job, consider signing up for an individual course or two.

Landmarks

If you are in your twenties . . . Your path to becoming a publicist is clear. If you are still in school, or could readily return to school, take courses in public relations. If your school does not offer them, take advantage of any course offerings in journalism, advertising, or marketing. You are in a good position at this age to apply for junior publicist positions. Experience will not matter so much at this entry level, but bear in mind that the pay is low, usually around $10 per hour.

If you are in your thirties or forties . . . You have probably read the above section and thought, "Wait a minute—I do not have any experience in PR, but I cannot afford to take a position for $10 per hour to get my foot in the door." That is understandable, but you do have other options, such as doing some local volunteer PR work in your spare time to build up your résumé. Also bear in mind that publicity is a trend-sensitive field. Do not give your potential clients any reason to wonder if you are hip enough for the job.

If you are in your fifties . . . Much depends upon your financial means and ability to leave your current job. If you have no relevant experience, then you are going to need to take some courses or devote considerable time to working for free before anyone will hire you as a publicist. Your age will not be a barrier if you have energy and connections.

If you are over sixty . . . Remember that a publicist works long hours, including many evenings and weekends, and the work requires tremendous energy and drive. Some employers may be skeptical that applicants over sixty have these qualities in sufficient abundance, so you may have to work twice as hard to assure them that you can handle the workload. If you have had a media-related career and can bring connections and relevant skills to your new position, your way will be smoother.

Further Resources

Publicist Jobs.com contains resources and career opportunities exclusively for publicists. http://www.publicistjobs.com

Mediabistro This media-oriented job site has extensive listings for publicist vacancies. http://www.mediabistro.com/publicist-jobs.html

Google Press Center is an archive of press releases. A publicist's main job duty is writing press releases, so it is a good idea to read a lot of them to get a sense of the proper form and tone. http://www.google.com/press

Universal Accreditation Board is a certification body for public relations specialists. Studies cited by the board show that accreditation increases earnings and marketability. http://www.praccreditation.org

Researcher

Researcher

Career Compasses

Get your bearings on what it takes to be a successful researcher.

Relevant Knowledge of the policy area that you are researching (30%)

Organizational Skills to track and present your research in a methodical fashion (30%)

Communication Skills to convey your findings (10%)

Mathematical Skills are useful, especially if your research is highly quantitative (30%)

Destination: Researcher

Many researchers work for universities. Their duties often include teaching undergraduate and graduate students, and supervising the research of degree candidates at all levels. The institution that employs them may fund some of their research, but much of their research funding will come from outside sources, foundations and the government primarily, which they will have applied for with grant applications. The process of grant writing is long and arduous. Universities usually have administrators that help academics with the grant-application process, and who administer the funds once the institution receives them. They act as an extra quality-control apparatus, helping to provide accountability to the donor, ensuring that the funds are spent in a manner consistent with the grant's stipulations, and offering the researcher relief from some of the administrative paperwork associated with research accountability and tax and other legal obligations. The necessity of bringing in funding to their department puts pressure on academic researchers that can be quite stressful. It is a continual cycle of applying for funding and providing accountability to your funders by documenting your progress, juggling it with teaching and administrative duties. If you are unable to bring in outside funding or get your work published, you are unlikely to retain your position at the university. The idea of bringing in money for your employer to pay your salary keep your job is a bit difficult to comprehend for those outside academia, who think that professors are paid for teaching out of the tuition paid by students. In fact, tuition covers only a tiny portion of the costs of higher education and research funding is crucial to the viability of most universities.

Essential Gear

Your degree is your passport to a new career. As you prepare your application packs for potential employers, consider copying your degree certificates and including them with your other application materials. Advanced degrees from prestigious universities are the currency used to obtain research positions, especially at the entry level before you have built up a record of your work that speaks for itself. Your education should be the first thing listed on your CV, at the top of the first page before your experience, professional memberships, and publications. Where you went to school, and what degrees you received there, are the primary pieces of information sought by potential employers and, to a lesser extent, research-funding bodies. By including copies of your degree certificates, you highlight this important feature of your credentials.

Newly minted Ph.D.s start out as assistant professors. They have six years to prove that they can bring in funding and get their work published. There are rarely reprieves or extensions; if they do not prove themselves as a researcher in six years, they get fired. If they succeed in impressing the tenure committee, they become associate professors. Later in their careers, if they have made significant contributions to their discipline, they can be named full professors or even obtain an endowed chair. This does not happen to all or even most tenured faculty and is a sign of prestige in one's field. Not all academics are tenure-track, however; some obtain one-year lectureships to fill temporary vacancies caused by professors going on sabbatical. These positions can be called *visiting lecturer, visiting researcher*, or *visiting professor*. There are post-doctoral research positions available at many major universities for recent Ph.D.s to gain some research experience while seeking tenure-track positions and preparing their first articles for publication. Varieties of other arrangements are available for academics to attach themselves to institutions in various ways, but the gold standard is the tenure-track position.

Academic researchers often work with one another on interdisciplinary research projects, apply jointly for funding for such projects, and hire and supervise research assistants. There is a stereotype of academics toiling alone in laboratories and libraries, but this is rarely the case today as research becomes larger-scale and more collaborative. Academics write up their research results in the form of academic papers that they present at conferences. Research results also appear in the form of articles in academic journals. When articles are submitted for publication, they are reviewed by other researchers in the same discipline, usually anonymously. This peer review helps ensure the quality of articles that are published since other researchers with the same expertise can spot flaws in the design, execution, or conclusions of the research project. Some research gets published in book form. Often a researcher's articles will appear first, which provides momentum for a publisher to accept the manuscript. If you cannot get an article published in a recognized journal in your field, it is unlikely that a publisher will take a risk publishing your work as a book. Today, there is a growing genre of crossover works in which researchers put their findings in a form that is palatable and digestible to the layperson outside their discipline. This type of work is prominent in the hard sciences, social sciences, history, and even literature. It is a way for researchers to reach beyond the ivory tower to find a wider audience for their work.

Another way that academic researchers seek to expand the usefulness of their work is by disseminating it to policy makers in government. Research grants can come from governments at all levels— local, state, and federal. The federal government is the largest funder of research. More specifically, academic researchers can be tapped to serve directly as government research consultants. This can sometimes require the professor to take a leave of absence from her or his home institution and temporarily move to Washington, D.C. For other consultant jobs, academics can be asked to prepare reports or provide expertise on specific public policy projects. It is not unusual for a top public policy researcher to be asked to fly to Washington for a meeting in the White House regarding a public policy initiative in his or her field. When you hear of the government exploring policy options in a given issue area, it is often, depending upon the disposition of the administration, consulting prominent academics in that policy area. To have your work actually make a difference in the real world as opposed to being buried in a niche journal with high prestige but little readership is the goal of many academic researchers but it is not easily obtained.

Essential Gear

Publish, publish, publish. Grantmakers and other funders of research like to have some reassurance that the recipients of their largesse will produce good work. Likewise research institutions such as universities and think tanks want to hire researchers with a track record of getting their work published in peer-reviewed journals. One way they do this is by looking carefully at the list of publications on an applicants CV. Be certain to list all of your articles, book chapters, books, book reviews, conference presentations, and any pending articles or manuscripts that are currently under review.

Researchers who desire to be more directly involved in public policy can work for other types of organizations outside of academia. Private sector corporations conduct extensive research and development in their industries and hire many researchers. The possible downside is that industry-sponsored research is often biased. A prime example is research on the health effects of smoking funded by tobacco companies. Ethics are not always equal to preventing sponsors from suppressing unfavorable results and tweaking research to obtain what they want to see. Your credibility as a researcher may be suspect if you become involved in some types of industry-sponsored research. On the other hand, there has been lifesaving research funded by industries that stood to make a profit from the drugs or devices or procedures that they nursed through research and development. It is up to you to decide if a private sector research position is right for you.

Nonprofit organizations are also often accused to biasing research to fit their ideological goals. The motive for bias in the private sector is clearly profit. In the nonprofit sector, the motivation is to produce research that backs up their preexisting policy preferences. Rarely are nonprofits neutral as to the outcome of their research, but certainly not all are unscrupulous about the conduct of their research. Again, it is a judgment call predicated on the individual organization and research project.

Finally, researchers are often employed at so-called think tanks. These are stand-alone research organizations. They are usually nonprofit, and they almost always claim to be nonpartisan, although they all have a strong conservative or liberal bias. Researchers employed in think tanks devote all of their time to research; they have no teaching duties.

You Are Here

You can begin your journey to researching from many different locales.

Are you an academic? The easiest career segue into research is from academia. Academics possess the requisite degrees and research skills. You may think that academics are primarily teachers, but professors at major research universities spend relatively little time teaching compared to conducting their research and writing activities. Academia rewards groundbreaking research and prominent publications; the atmosphere at most colleges and universities is often described as "publish or perish" due to the fact that tenure is dependent upon publishing your research in book and article form. Academics rely primarily on outside research grants to fund their work. Since much research funding comes from the government, you can become a researcher without changing the source of your livelihood per se.

Do you have an advanced degree? Most research jobs require at least a master's degree, with a doctorate the preferred degree level for most positions. With an undergraduate degree, especially one in the discipline in which you intend to do research—for example, a political science major who has taken statistics courses might apply for a public policy research position—you could secure an internship or entry-level research assistant position, but you would need to earn an advanced degree to move up the career ladder.

Do you have grant-writing experience? Securing money to conduct research is half the battle. Once you have the funding, the real work begins; but obtaining that funding is often a large and stressful part of a researcher's job. There is an art to framing your research proposals so that they appeal to potential funders. It is a different skill set from the research itself. If you do not have grant-writing experience, you may want to take a course. There are many grant-writing workshops around the country, including an increasing number conducted online. Remember to check references before you fork over any money for a grant-writing course, whether conducted online or in-person.

Organizing Your Expedition

Before you set out, know where you are going.

Decide on a destination. Researchers work in several types of institutions. Your research area, skills, experience, and interests will help guide you to the right one for you. Your ability to transition from your current career to becoming a full-time researcher depends primarily on your education. Degrees are more important than experience in obtaining research positions. Employers are looking for applicants who have been socialized into the discipline via their educational background, who have conducted research at school, learned how to write academic papers and present them at conferences, and who have taken appropriate courses in research methods. Beyond your degrees, you will need to consider your research interests. Do you want to be involved with research that is conducted by the public, private, or nonprofit sector? Do you want to teach as well or conduct research exclusively? How direct a connection to public policy do you want your research to have?

Scout the terrain. The next logical step is considering what research jobs are available in your locality. Do you live in or near our nation's capital? Most think tanks are based in Washington, D.C. Other major cities, such as New York and San Francisco, contain the headquarters of some think tanks and nonprofit research entities. Obviously, if you are looking for an academic research position, you need to be near a major research university. Corporate research parks are spread throughout the country,

Navigating the Terrain

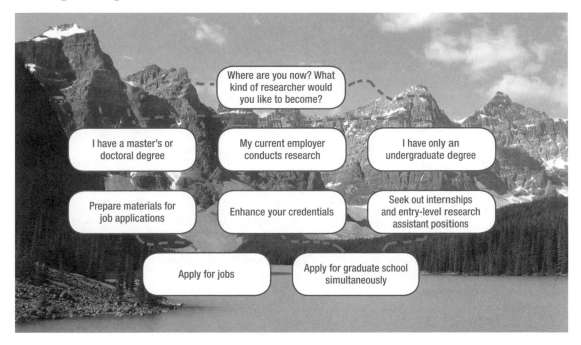

and some are far removed from major metropolitan areas. If you do not live near the type of institution where you would like to work, you need to assess your ability and willingness to move for the right position.

Find the path that's right for you. This career change is particularly tricky to discuss because the ability to make the transition into research is so heavily dependent upon your educational background. Most of the careers in this series are geared toward the motivated career changer who is prepared to take some courses or obtain certification in a new field, but careers that require specific and lengthy degrees such as law or medicine are excluded. Researcher may seem like a bit of an exception, but there are many people who do not currently work in the field in which they obtained their degree. This is particularly true in the social sciences, where people with degrees in political science, sociology, or related fields may have unrelated jobs. If you are longing to work in the discipline of your degree, you are a prime candidate for a career change into research. Use the resources in this chapter to pinpoint the type of research position that is right for you.

Notes from the Field
Carri Ferrand
Research assistant, Brady Campaign to Prevent Gun Violence
Boston, Massachusetts

What were you doing before you decided to change careers?
I was working for a democratic political polling firm as a junior analyst and data programmer.

Why did you change your career?
Essentially, I was grossly underpaid and overworked in the political world. There was never any down time at the polling firm because we worked not only on domestic political campaigns but also on international campaigns and other corporate projects. Going into the nonprofit/academic research world was much slower paced—but I was able to also use my statistics background. It seemed to make sense at the time.

Go back to school. Research is not a field that you can usually enter without an advanced degree. A few lower-level research assistant positions may be available for applicants with an undergraduate degree but applicants for these posts are usually in the process of obtaining graduate degrees. If you only have a BA or BS, your first move career change-oriented move will be going back to school. There are many resources to help you choose a graduate program that fits your needs and interests. *U.S. News and World Report* ranks graduate research programs by discipline, and its rankings are widely accepted as broadly accurate indications of quality and prestige.

Landmarks

If you are in your twenties . . . There are specific steps you can take to get yourself into a career in research. The first step involves obtaining at least a master's degree and, ideally, a doctorate in the area in which you intend to do research. The next step entails getting your foot in the door

How did you make the transition?

I certainly had to get used to the slower pace and learn to meet dead-lines in a different way. When you are constantly going and balancing multiple projects, it is easier for me to stay on track and stay focused. The research projects at the Brady Campaign were more long-term projects. I was still able to use my experience and education in polling and statistics and apply that to our research projects—which in essence were geared toward using crime data to push for change in the gun laws.

What are the keys to success in your new career?

Lean on your strengths, past experience, and knowledge. It is important to find ways to apply the experience you have to your new position—if you can. For me, once I mastered the pace of my new position, the work fell into place.

at your think tank of choice. You can do this by looking for entry-level research assistant positions and by looking for internships.

If you are in your thirties or forties . . . You might already be a researcher. Seriously. Even if you are not directly employed in conducting public policy or other research, you might be working for a grant-funded public, private, or nonprofit organization that is conducting research in some capacity. Your first move then is to inquire about how you could make an internal transfer to be more directly involved in research with your current employer.

If you are in your fifties . . . You are entering a field where experience is valued and respect comes with a lengthy CV. You are unlikely to face age discrimination in the hiring process unless you are transferring from an entirely unrelated field into an entry-level research job that normally employs twenty-something graduate assistants. Even then, returning to school at an older age for advanced degrees is becoming more common so you are not likely to be the only nontraditional researcher or student at your institution.

If you are over sixty . . . Your career change strategy needs to draw on the skills and experience that you have obtained thus far on your career journey. You can still go back to school for a degree in the field in which you would like to conduct research, but take advantage of any opportunities to get involved with research immediately to make connections and bolster your CV.

Further Resources

Resources for the Future is a public policy think tank based in Washington, D.C., that focuses on environmental and natural resource policymaking. http://www.rff.org

American Enterprise Institute for Public Policy Research is a conservative think tank based in Washington, D.C. http://www.aei.org

RAND Corporation is a large and well-funded research institution, founded in the post-WWII era with an initial focus on security issues that has since expanded to encompass virtually all public policy areas. Site includes job listings. http://www.rand.org

Association for Institutional Research is a membership organization for institutional researchers that includes job listings. They specialize in research to improve postsecondary institutions, which is a niche area, but a large one with many job opportunities. http://www.airweb.org

Legal Advisor

Legal Advisor

Career Compasses

Get your bearings on what it takes to be a successful legal advisor.

Relevant Knowledge of the law in your area of specialization (30%)

Organizational Skills will keep you on top of your workload (20%)

Communication Skills are necessary to deal with a variety of people in your work, especially when dealing with controversial issues (30%)

Ability to Manage Stress is always useful when dealing with the vagaries of politics and law (20%)

Destination: Legal Advisor

When you saw the title of this chapter, you may have thought, "I pay my lawyer for legal advice. Isn't that what a lawyer does?" Yes, a "legal advisor" is an attorney, and all lawyers are in the business of giving legal advice to their clients. It can be a bit confusing to distinguish the career of legal advisor from other types of legal practice. Let us first look at where legal advisor fits into the array of career options open to lawyers. Some lawyers work as professors of law at law schools. They may be called upon to give legal advice on a consultative basis, but they usually do not actively practice law, contributing instead by training future lawyers and writing scholarly books and articles on law and legal history. Some lawyers become judges in local, state, or federal courts. Technically, one does not have to possess a law degree to become a judge, but the law has become so complex that it is unheard of for a non-lawyer to be selected for a judgeship today. Likewise, many public officials are lawyers by degree, as are a good number of entrepreneurs, but legal training is not required for these fields; it just makes a good background. For the same reasons, these fields are where legal advisors work. Legal advisors help clients fit their plans to a legal landscape, sometimes working to change the landscape itself.

Consider the diverse ways of being a lawyer to grasp the scope of the legal advisor's terrain. Most lawyers work for private law firms or go into private practice for themselves. There are many areas of specialization that a lawyer can choose, including corporate law, which includes mergers and acquisitions, copyright, patent and trade law, intellectual property, trusts and estates, personal injury, contracts, real estate, family law, such as divorce and custody issues, and criminal law, among others. Defense lawyers can work in private practice or they can work for the government as public defenders. The federal government and state governments hire lawyers to work as both prosecutors and defense attorneys. Most government agencies have a substantial legal team, especially those agencies that are concerned with finding and prosecuting financial fraud, such as the Securities and Exchange Commission (SEC) and the U.S. Commodities Futures Trading Commission (CFTC), not to mention the Department of Justice and the IRS.

Essential Gear

Wear your passion on your sleeve. Most nonprofit organizations are ideologically committed to their policy goals. They are passionate about the environment, human rights, civil rights, civil liberties, reproductive rights or whatever their area of concentration. They are not going to hire someone who does not appear to personally share their political views and policy orientation. No matter how skillful or experienced you are, a nonprofit is not going to hire you if they do not trust your commitment to their issue. This so-called "cause lawyering" is different from other types of legal work where it does not matter what you personally think of your client.

The nonprofit sector employs many lawyers, too. Nonprofit organizations work to change public policies by grassroots activism, protests, lobbying, boycotts, and many other tactics, but today they mainly work for policy change through the courts. There are several ways that they can do this. One method is by arranging test cases, that is, someone deliberately breaks a law in order to challenge its constitutionality. The legal arm of the nonprofit with the goal of instituting this policy change defends the lawbreaker and, if they succeed in pleading their case, gets the court to nullify the law in question or alter its meaning favorably. One prominent example is the famous case of *Griswold v. Connecticut* (1965), in which Estelle Griswold got herself arrested dispensing birth control to challenge a state law prohibiting the use of birth control by married couples. Lawyers for her organization, the Planned Parenthood League of Connecticut, defended her case up to the Supreme Court, and she succeeded in getting the Connecticut statute overturned as a violation of a constitutional right to privacy. The Griswold opinion created the legal groundwork for later cases concerning privacy rights such as *Roe v. Wade* (1973) and *Lawrence v. Texas* (2003). So, you can begin to see why nonprofits value test cases as a policy change strategy.

Essential Gear

Get some experience in the trenches. When you hire someone to give you advice, you expect them to be an expert, to possess specialized knowledge that is worth its price. If you are a young, inexperienced lawyer or one who is seeking to make a radical change from your previous legal work, you might bolster your résumé by gaining some volunteer experience in your new field. Most nonprofits are eager to have attorneys who will do pro bono work for them and such work could lead to a job offer in the future.

Another way that nonprofits accomplish this same goal is by taking up the defense of ordinary citizens who are accused of breaking a law with which the organization disagrees. The outcome and defense are the same as in a test case, except that these cases are not created to test the law. A prominent example here would be *Brandenburg v. Ohio* (1969). Clarence Brandenburg, a local Ku Klux Klan leader, was arrested for advocating violence in a speech at a rally. With the assistance of the ACLU, he pleaded his case up to the Supreme Court, who declared that speech, no matter how hateful, vile, or inflammatory, is protected by the First

Amendment unless it leads to "imminent lawless action." This precedent is still in effect today. Due to the principle of stare decisis (standing by prior decisions), lower courts are obliged to respect higher court precedent, giving a long life to these decisions.

Finally, lawyers for nonprofits can file amicus curiae briefs in cases in which they are not involved in hopes of persuading the judges to their interpretation of the law. All of these strategies are predicated on the idea that judges make law as much as legislators. Traditionally, if you want a law changed, you lobby the legislature, attempting to get a bill considered and voted upon, and influencing the language of that bill. Certainly lawyers work as lobbyists, and lawyers for nonprofits and corporations are involved in writing policy, crafting the exact wording of new laws to suit their special interests. But recently there has been a growing understanding that, when a judge interprets a law, he or she is declaring what that law means on the ground, in practice. Laws are often written in vague language; they are subject to interpretation and application in particular situations. When a judge interprets a law in light of a particular case, he or she is, in effect, making law. Consider the supreme law of the land, the U.S. Constitution. The Bill of Rights provides protection for many civil liberties that American citizens hold dear. Although the ink has long since dried on the page, and the words have not been altered, the meaning of those civil liberties protections has changed over time. It has not changed due to the legislature making new laws to change the meaning of the Bill of Rights; it has changed due to the courts. To illustrate, ponder the Fourth Amendment protection against "unreasonable search and seizure" or the Eighth Amendment prohibition against "cruel and unusual punishment." What search is unreasonable? What punishment is cruel? It is up to the judges of each era to make that determination, and the meaning is not static; it changes with new cases and new judges, who are influenced by the social mores of their day. This is why nonprofits have looked in recent times toward the courts rather than the legislature to further their policy goals, and this is where legal advisors come in. Legal advisors are lawyers employed by the legal arms of nonprofits to assist them in achieving their policy aims through the use of the courts. Private industry can also employ legal advisors, but since this volume is geared toward nonprofits and government jobs, we will mainly consider the employment of legal advisors by the nonprofit sector and the government.

You Are Here

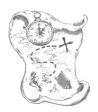

You can begin your journey to legal advising from many different locales.

Are you an attorney? Legal advising is a career option for lawyers. Non-lawyers may be able to find work as a legal assistant, researcher, or paralegal, but the job of legal advisor is reserved for applicants who possess a law degree. You will have to get a law degree is if you want this job. If you are already an attorney, segueing into a legal advisory role should be a fairly straightforward operation. Update your résumé and look to the resources at the end of this chapter for jobs.

Do you have an area of legal expertise? Legal advisors generally specialize in one area of law. It stands to reason that, in order to be able to give useful advice, you need to know a lot about the issue! Although there are legal advisors in every area of law, certain policy niches are more common. There is plenty of demand now, for example, for human

Navigating the Terrain

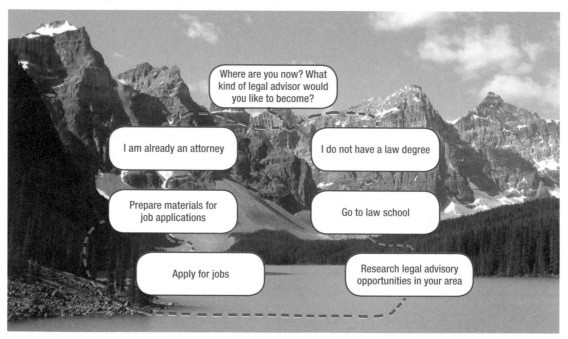

rights law and this is likely to remain a growing field. Environmental law as it relates to public health has been a significant area, and there are plenty of opportunities for advising nonprofits on their own governance, due to the complexity of rules for incorporation, charitable giving, political contributions, taxes, and other operations shaped by intricate laws.

Do you have connections in the nonprofit sector or within the government? This is no more or less true for legal advising than any other job search, but it helps to know someone in your desired field. If, in your previous legal work, you have had any nonprofits or government agencies for clients, you may want to alert them to the fact that you are now seeking full-time legal advising work. If they are not currently hiring, they may keep you in mind for future vacancies, alert you to openings of which they are aware, or hire you part-time or on a project basis.

Organizing Your Expedition

Before you set out, know where you are going.

Decide on a destination. You can work as a legal advisor for either the private or nonprofit sectors as well as the government. The private sector usually has organizations representing industry that lobby on that industry's behalf. These organizations, rather than the companies in that industry, are the first place to look for jobs. The American Bar Association, for example, lobbies for legislation favorable to the interests of lawyers. The American Medical Association does the same for doctors. If you want to make a lot of money, look for lucrative industries, such as the energy and telecommunications sectors. Also consider the career of lobbyist. Many lobbyists are attorneys, and the lines between legal advisors and lobbyists can sometimes blur. Federal, state, and local governments all employ legal advisors, but the most jobs are at the federal level. Most federal agencies have a team of legal advisors, so if you would like the security and benefits of a civil service job, consider working for the federal government. The greater opportunity for the second careerist is in the broad array of legal advisor opportunities found in the nonprofit sector. Virtually all nonprofits over a minimum size employ legal advisors; they need them to mount effective challenges to existing policies and to write

Stories from the Field

Jon Choon Yoo
Legal advisor, U.S. Justice Department Office of Legal Counsel
Washington, D.C.

John Yoo is a professor of law at the Boalt Hall School of Law, University of California, Berkeley. He is well-known for his ultra-conservative legal views and he became famous (or infamous) as one of the authors of the USA PATRIOT Act when he was employed by the Justice Department as a legal advisor to President Bush from 2001-2003. He has since been employed as a visiting scholar at the American Enterprise Institute, a conservative think tank. He has made a name for himself in conservative legal circles by crafting memos in which he asserts the legality of torture as well as explaining how, in his view, enemy combatants can be denied the protections of the Geneva Convention. He has also asserted a theory of a unitary presidency, and provided legal advice on the issue of warrantless wiretapping that gives broad authority to the executive branch.

Yoo was born in South Korea but was raised in Philadelphia, Pennsylvania. He attended Harvard University as an undergraduate, followed by Yale Law School. He secured a prestigious Supreme Court clerkship for Justice Clarence Thomas, and also clerked for the D. C. Circuit. He served as general counsel for the Senate Judiciary Committee before obtaining his current professorship at Berkeley. He is an active and prominent member of the Federalist Society. Yoo's scholarly work was

the laws they desire, not to mention to defend victims of laws that they consider to be discriminatory. So, your first task is to determine whether your skills and interests would find a better fit within the private, public, or nonprofit sectors. The next question to ask yourself is what area of specialization suits you.

Scout the terrain. The easiest place to begin a job search journey is in your own backyard. Unless you have a strong desire to move, look first for legal advisor vacancies in your locality. Most jobs are going to be concentrated around major cities, where corporations, nonprofits, and government agencies have offices. Washington, D.C., has by far the highest *controversial for its defense of unilateral executive power, especially in reference to war, and these writings certainly helped him obtain his legal advisor position in the Bush administration.*

During his tenure under former Attorney General Alberto Gonzales, Yoo was the author of a number of memos, some still classified, that gave legal authority to the Bush administration's strategies and tactics in the so-called War on Terror. Among the most controversial were his narrowly defining the habeas corpus obligations of the United States to detainees in the war; his advocacy of "enhanced interrogation techniques" as legally defensible; and his urging that the United States should refute the Geneva Convention to avoid U.S. officials being prosecuted under the War Crimes Act of 1996 due to their actions in the War on Terror, especially in Iraq. He is also known for asserting that the president has the legal power to authorize the National Security Administration (NSA) to monitor the telecommunications of U.S. citizens without a warrant and without violating the Fourth Amendment.

Whether or not you agree with Yoo's policy preferences and constitutional scholarship, the fact is that he has had a successful career as a prominent legal advisor at the highest levels of the federal government. He started out with good schools, secured a top shelf clerkship, and stayed with the federal government, moving into a professorship that will enable him to continue to do legal consulting on the side. His writings and his connections, as well as his school pedigree, all helped him to get a legal advising job.

concentration of legal advisory positions in the country. New York and San Francisco also have a fair number in all three sectors, as well as state-oriented opportunities. Other major cities will have a scattering of corporate or nonprofits headquarters, although there are likely to be fewer federal government jobs outside of regional headquarters for agencies like the IRS and EPA.

Find the path that's right for you. That means taking an honest and insightful look at your skills and interests, and doing some research into whether the sort of legal advising position you want is available in your area. If it is not, you have to consider whether you are willing to move to make this career change happen. If you cannot or will not move, do not give up. Technology has made telecommuting an option for legal advising, and you may be able to apply for a job based in Washington, D.C., even if you are based in St. Louis, Missouri.

Go back to school. If you possess a law degree, there is no further degree or certification requirement that you need, except that you will need to pass the bar in whichever state your new legal advising job is located. If you lack a law degree, you are going to have to go to law school in order to pursue this career change. Law school normally takes three years full-time, but many law schools allow you to attend evening classes so you can pursue a law degree part-time around your current job.

Landmarks

If you are in your twenties . . . If you have completed law school, you can simply turn to the job ads and apply for legal advisor positions. Your lack of experience will disqualify you from some jobs where the potential employer is seeking an experienced litigator in a certain policy area, but you should easily be able to get your foot in the door in whichever of the three sectors interests you. Be prepared to work very hard and conduct a lot of research. If you learn the ropes at a bootstrapped nonprofit, you may face a lot of grunt work from more-experienced legal advisors, but you will move up the ranks and have a lot of responsibility quickly.

If you are in your thirties or forties . . . Once again, the process is straightforward if you are a lawyer: just update your résumé, look for jobs that interest you, and apply. Play up the relevance of your previous legal experience in your cover letter. If you want to move in to a different legal area, tell your prospective employer why they should hire you. You will need to sell yourself in your application if you have been a patent attorney and you want to move into human rights law.

If you are in your fifties . . . Your years of experience as a lawyer will lend credibility and weight to your application. You should be welcomed in most any sector, provided that you have the ability to demonstrate why you are qualified to dispense legal advice in that particular policy area.

Stick as close as possible to what you know already, and your chances of success will increase. Remember, sell yourself in that cover letter. Why should nonprofit X take legal advice from you? Do not assume it is obvious—tell them!

If you are over sixty . . . There is not much that distinguishes your application from those in the fifties age group, except that some legal advisory roles are time-consuming, emotionally draining, involve intense research, and lots of travel. Be sure to impress upon potential employers that you have the energy and drive to do the job. If you are concerned about not spreading yourself too thin, part-time opportunities are abundant in this legal advising.

Further Resources

Idealist.org is one of the main online sources of nonprofit job listings, including legal advisor positions. http://www.idealist.org

American Civil Liberties Union is a national nonprofit organization with chapters in every state that fights for the upholding of civil liberties embodied in the Constitution. http://www.aclu.org

NAACP Legal Defense Fund is the section of the National Association for the Advancement of Colored People that provides legal assistance to poor African Americans. http://www.naacpldf.org

Earthjustice Legal Defense Fund is the new name for the Sierra Club Legal Defense Fund. It is based in Washington, D.C., but has eight offices around the country, including one for international programs in Oakland, California. http://www.earthjustice.org

Volunteer
Coordinator

Volunteer Coordinator

Career Compasses

Get your bearings on what it takes to be a successful volunteer coordinator.

Relevant Knowledge of how to herd cats—that is, manage volunteers (25%)

Organizational Skills are crucial to efficient management of personnel (25%)

Communication Skills are useful for dealing with your volunteers and colleagues (25%)

Caring about the work of your organization is motivating and will not be lost on your volunteers (25%)

Destination: Volunteer Coordinator

The career of volunteer coordinator stands out from the others in this volume for the stark reason that it is often an unpaid position. Volunteer coordinators are frequently volunteers themselves. On political campaigns and other time-sensitive projects, people volunteer their time for short periods for a cause that motivates them to put in hours above and beyond their regular jobs. This flexibility increases your opportunities to serve in this capacity, but reduces its viability as a career-change option.

Although, let us be quick to add that some volunteer coordinators are paid, either on a per-project basis or in full-time or part-time salaried positions with benefits. The pay is not high, but museums and other nonprofit organizations that rely regularly on volunteers usually have a paid staff member who manages them. This is probably the sort of position you have in mind if you are considering a career move into this field. This chapter focuses mainly on volunteer coordinators who are paid staff members in their organizations, but bear in mind that short-term, unpaid volunteer coordinator positions may help you build the credentials to get a paying job down the road.

What does a volunteer coordinator do? The job duties vary based on the size of the organization, the type of work it does, and the scope of the activities that involve volunteers. To start, a good volunteer coordinator maintains a list of tasks that can be done by volunteers and continually augments it with new and creative ways that volunteers can be utilized. These tasks can include distributing leaflets or posting fliers; selling raffle or event tickets; ushering or providing security and ticket-taking or checking services; stuffing envelopes and other tasks associated with mailings; packing items for shipping; opening and processing mail, especially donations; and fundraising, particularly by telephone. Volunteers with special skills can often be called upon for various professional services. A Web designer, for example, might volunteer his or her time designing and maintaining a Web site for a nonprofit organization whose work he or she supports. A medical professional might volunteer to be on-call for emergencies at an event, a caterer might donate food, or a printer might donate copying services. These are just a few examples of the many types of professional services that can be donated, and a volunteer coordinator needs to be able to solicit these contributions and coordinate with the people and companies providing the service. Volunteer coordinators consider the whole

Essential Gear

Walk your talk. If you have not volunteered, organizations are going to wonder about your qualifications and motivation for leading other volunteers. So, accumulate a record of volunteering and put this experience on your résumé and into your cover letters when you apply for volunteer coordinator positions. Also bear in mind that volunteering can serve as a stepping-stone to a leadership role. In fact, volunteering is the best way to get a job as a volunteer coordinator, so get out there and volunteer.

of an organization's expenses and think of ways to obtain some necessary services by way of volunteers, or at least at a substantial discount. There is no limit to the type of work that can be done by volunteers, and some nonprofit organizations, such as animal shelters, frequently have no paid staff at all. Legal services can be donated on a pro bono basis, as can tax preparation and other accounting services. A savvy volunteer coordinator will know how to work all of the connections within the organization's membership and leadership. Is there a Certified Public Accountant on the board? Perhaps a polite inquiry about donating some time outside of the traditionally hectic tax season might save the organization some money and get tasks like tax preparation out of the way early. In order to assess an organization's needs for volunteers, a volunteer coordinator must communicate effectively with all of the different areas within the organization. Being able to ask about their needs, and really listen to what they say, is a critical skill. A related task is letting different units know how volunteers might be able to assist them in ways they had not thought of previously. A good volunteer coordinator is always considering ways to use volunteers more effectively. In addition to reaching out within the organization, it is necessary to let the public know what volunteer opportunities are available. Often people are eager to volunteer but do not know what volunteer opportunities will fit their schedules, skills, and interests. As the first point of contact for volunteers, it is up to the coordinator to match potential volunteers with tasks that suit their abilities and schedule.

Dealing with actual volunteers is a major part of the job. Volunteer coordinators spend some of their working hours on solitary tasks like searching for best practices in volunteer management so they can integrate them into their organization, but the majority of their time is spent in hands-on coordination with volunteers. If you have ever volunteered and you needed to find the boss, you probably knew to look for the harried-looking person carrying the clipboard, checking people in and out, and passing out T-shirts, boxes of fliers, umbrellas, phone lists, or other paraphernalia for the job at hand. If you become a volunteer manager, this flustered, overworked person will be you. Do not let that put you off though, as the rewards for people who are united by a cause they believe in are many and they run deeper than your paycheck. Formally appreciating the volunteer staff is job duty of the volunteer coordinator. After an event or campaign, or during the holiday season, you will need to show

how you value the volunteers who have served your organization. Some-times volunteers receive T-shirts, tote bags, umbrellas, or other items with the organization's logo on it. Another option is to host a party for volunteers. If your organization has exhibits or holds concerts or other events, it is customary for volunteers to get free admission or member-ship as a reward for their efforts. Just as volunteer coordinators need to be create in how they utilize volunteers, they need to be equally creative in dreaming up ways to reward them that will not sap the organization's budget and that will encourage future volunteering.

Essential Gear

Give your organizational skills a check-up. Out of necessity, nonprofit organizations fre-quently give positions of responsibility, such as volunteer coordination, to whomever will take them. If you have worked with a nonprofit in any capacity, you will know that this unfortu-nate state of affairs can sometimes have disas-trous results. For every superb organizer, there are three well-intentioned but completely clue-less people who try their best but have gotten in over their heads. Do not be one of those people. Read books on organization, take a course in organizational skills, or practice orga-nizing events for your family to be sure that your organizational abilities are up to the job. You want to make a good impression and have your efforts rewarded with future job offers.

Let us consider a specific example of a paid professional volunteer coordinator to gain further insight into the day-to-day tasks. Equine Affaire is a four-day equine educational exhibition that takes place an-nually in three locations: Cali-fornia, Ohio, and Massachusetts. It features a trade show, clin-ics, seminars, demonstrations, competitive events, events and exhibits just for children, hun-dreds of vendors of equine-re-lated products and services, and an evening spectacular called the Fantasia. Every aspect of the setup, cleanup, day-to-day oper-ations and evening programs is conducted by volunteers. Volunteers receive free admission for each day on which they volunteer at least two hours of their time. Ushers for the Fantasia get to see this always-sold-out spectacle and get a free T-shirt in the bargain. There is also a raffle for special prizes for volunteers. The volunteer coordinator for Equine Affaire travels to all three events and spends the entire year securing volunteers and arranging the logistics of local volunteer coordination at each event with a team of subordinates based in each region. Pulling off the event with hundreds of volunteering doing everything from selling tickets to setting up jumps in the arena takes an incredible amount of coordination and stellar organizational skills.

You Are Here

You can begin your journey to volunteer coordination from many different locales.

Have you worked in human resources? Coordinating volunteers is not the same as managing the hiring, firing, compensation and benefits of paid employees, but there are enough similarities that HR experience or educational background might help you make this career change. Likewise, if you have managed employees, projects, departments, teams, or acted as a leader or coach for a sports team, youth group, or had any similar experience directing people, you will find that useful in your new role and you should emphasize it on your résumé and in your cover letter when you apply for jobs.

Do you have any volunteering experience? It stands to reason that you will be a more effective volunteer coordinator if you know what it feels like from the other side. If you have volunteered in situations where leadership was disorganized, details were forgotten, and planning seemed to be absent, make a note of what mistakes not to make. On the other hand, if you have witnessed effective volunteer coordination, incorporate the best practices you have observed into your own work.

Do you have a connection to a particular cause? If you have an undergraduate or graduate degree in art history or social work or environmental economics but you have not put it to use in your current career (and you do not really see what jobs are open to you in your field), give volunteer coordination some thought as a possible compromise. For the art history example, you could coordinate volunteers in a museum. Although you would not be working with the art on the walls per se, you would be steeped in an environment that would be aesthetically appealing to you, and you would be performing a necessary function to keep the appreciation of art and its history alive.

Navigating the Terrain

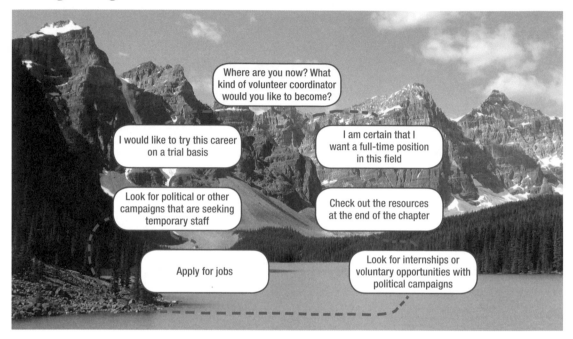

Organizing Your Expedition

Before you set out, know where you are going.

Decide on a destination. As you begin your journey to your new career, remember that there are a variety of ways that you can test the waters before plunging in full-time. If you register as a member of a political party, or contribute to a political candidate, you will begin to receive solicitations for volunteering your time to campaigns. The same thing may happen when you contribute to a nonprofit organization such as a museum, animal shelter, or environmental cause group. When you follow-up on one of these solicitations, make it known that you are seeking a leadership role. You will go through a more substantial vetting process to become a volunteer coordinator than to simply volunteer, as the organization will want to know your qualifications and experience in volunteer leadership. This is the time to point out that you lead your daughter's Girl Scout troop, coach your son's soccer team, or supervise a department of eight.

Scout the terrain. The first step toward becoming a volunteer coordinator is becoming a volunteer. Wherever you live, volunteer opportunities will exist, and every opportunity means that there is someone coordinating those volunteers. Look for requests for volunteers put out by organizations in your community, and call them to find out if they are looking for volunteer coordinators. If they are not searching at present, then sign up as a volunteer. If you learn the ropes, get to know the organization's staff, and make a good impression, you will be in a good position to take advantage of any future vacancies that arise. This is not the sort of career for which one would usually contemplate a major move, but look online for jobs in other cities and states if you are motivated to relocate for the right position.

Find the path that's right for you. The steps that you will take on your journey to your new career in volunteer management depend upon whether you are looking for a full-time, salaried position—or you would be satisfied with a part-time, temporary or unpaid role in this field? The former type is the hardest to find, but jobs are out there if you look hard enough and have patience. This career change may take longer than some others not because of the required degrees or experience but because so few volunteer coordinator positions are full-time careers. You may need to plan on holding onto your current job for an indefinite period as you search for vacancies and gain experience in your new field. With time and diligent searching, the right job for you will materialize.

Go back to school. It is unlikely that you would go back to school to become a volunteer coordinator, or even that you would need to take individual courses. A management-related degree would be helpful, especially one geared toward a career in human resources or, of course, nonprofit management. But most jobs are unlikely to be so picky as to require a specific degree. They will be more concerned about your experience, your organizational skills, and your enthusiasm.

Landmarks

If you are in your twenties . . . You can probably guess what to do next: volunteer! If you are still in school, take advantage of any courses that your school offers in nonprofit or personnel management, and highlight

Notes from the Field

Gloria French
Director of development and
   community relations, Plymouth Place Senior Living
Boston, Massachusetts

What were you doing before you decided to change careers?

I had a fairly lengthy career as a middle-school teacher. I taught mathematics, language arts, and social studies. I interrupted my career briefly to raise my children when they were small, but went back to teaching when they started school.

Why did you change your career?

I had taken a job with a new school district, and I was not rehired along with the rest of the new teachers that year. Also, after several years of being out of full-time teaching, I did not like the changes that occurred—much less autonomy and creativity.

How did you make the transition?

My being let go was a blessing in disguise because my mother-in-law's health was failing, and we discovered she had pancreatic cancer. My

them in your cover letter and résumé, but do not feel obliged to change majors to enter this field. Whether you are in school or not, pursue any volunteer leadership positions that appeal to you. If you like children, volunteer to coach a sports team, youth group, or scouting organization. Think about what you do well and lead groups doing it, whether it is nature hikes, trail rides or museum tours for tourists in French or Japanese.

If you are in your thirties or forties . . . You probably have some volunteering experience under your belt, and you may very well have some leadership experience by now, too. Update your résumé so that it showcases your relevant experience, and look for jobs that interest you. Do not give notice at your current job until you are certain that you can live on a volunteer coordinator's salary.

not working allowed us to have her in our house with hospice care for her last two months, and I was happy to be able to provide that for her. After her death, I looked into some other opportunities, one of which was to apply for training to become an Edward Jones Investments agent. However, a woman in my church knew that I was looking to make a change from teaching. She had worked at Plymouth Place and retired because of her husband's health, but had been called to come back to a new position of Community Relations Coordinator. She asked if I'd be interested and recommended me to the CEO. The job was a perfect fit and was an extension of volunteer work I'd done for a number of community organizations. A new CEO, who arrived 15 months after me, asked if I would take over development (fundraising), as well as continue volunteer coordination, and that worked out also.

What are the keys to success in your new career?

One of my keys to success has always been that I am willing to try something new. And most of the time, I have enjoyed the change—when I wouldn't have sought it out. I have strong people skills and a desire to help others succeed, be happy, and find the information that they need.

If you are in your fifties . . . Whatever career path you have followed up to now, even if it has been as a full-time parent, has probably provided you with experiences that will make you a desirable candidate for volunteer coordinator jobs. You need to consider whether the pay is sufficient. Consider moving gradually to identify your most satisfying involvement.

If you are over sixty . . . Like your colleagues who are in their fifties, your general life and work experience will make you a valuable asset to any organization. If you are retired, you may have the luxury of volunteering to coordinate volunteer services without worrying about the pay. Even if you are seeking a full-time paid position, you may be able to segue into it from unpaid work. Take advantage of connections you have made in your personal and professional life to find your first job in your new field.

Further Resources

Volunteer Match does just what its name implies: It matches volunteers with suitable opportunities. http://www.volunteermatch.org

NonProfitExpert.com is a site maintained by a nonprofit management consultant that provides educational resources for nonprofit organizations. http://www.nonprofitexpert.com

Idealist.org is a one-stop shop for information for nonprofit organizations. Contains extensive job listings, including thousands of volunteer and volunteer coordinator positions. http://www.idealist.org

TechSoup is a technology information site for nonprofits. This link goes to a useful articles titled, "Negotiating the Nonprofit-Volunteer Relationship: Making a Successful Match." http://www.techsoup.org/learningcenter/volunteers/page4894.cfm

Trainer

Career Compasses

Get your bearings on what it takes to be a successful trainer.

Relevant Knowledge of the business management skills that you are teaching (30%)

Organizational Skills to keep track of your clients and their needs (20%)

Communication Skills to impart knowledge effectively to clients (20%)

Ability to Manage Stress is crucial when you are a trainer as your work environment and your clients will vary from gig to gig (30%)

Destination: Trainer

When you hear the term *trainer*, you are probably looking for another word to put in front of it, such as dog trainer, horse trainer, or personal fitness trainer. Other equally ambiguous terms that are sometimes used for this field are "contract trainer," "consultant," or "coach." So, it seems like the first step on the path to becoming a trainer is to define exactly what type of trainer we are talking about here. We are not talking about getting buff at the gym. In the career sense, a trainer is someone who teaches employees to do their jobs more effectively. The majority of such trainers work in the corporate world, but a growing number serve the nonprofit and public sectors.

Trainers are not usually permanent employees of the offices in which they conduct training; rather, trainers work for training companies that hire them out on a temporary, contract basis to do on-site training, or they are self-employed as consultants who move from project to project as freelance contractors. Some very large organizations that train new employees in certain skills on a regular, recurring basis may employ permanent in-house consultants, but this is not the norm. The temporary nature of each contract means that trainers can sometimes go for long periods between jobs, so you may need a backup source of income, at least while you are building up a client base. But if you are looking to make a slow segue from your current career, working part-time as a trainer might suit you perfectly.

A trainer is really a teacher, and what you can teach depends upon what you know. Corporate trainers teach management-level employees business leadership and financial management techniques that can cover anything from how to work with budgets to negotiation and mediation techniques to how to be a good boss. As employees climb the corporate ladder, their new performance expectations may not be a good match for their existing skills and experience. They may find that being good at their previous job, which got them the promotion, does not mean that they can now manage people or projects or large budgets. Trainers work to build "soft" interpersonal skills as much as "hard" job skills. A trainer could be hired to teach basic interpersonal skills such as how to communicate effectively, how to listen, how to negotiate the PC minefield of diversity in the workplace, how to be assertive, and how to deal with

Essential Gear

Reel in and mount your credentials. The certification requirements for trainers will vary, depending upon whether you are training in a soft area of employee performance enhancement or something very specialized such as a particular software program. Training companies may have specific degree and certification requirements for their trainers, but if you decide to venture out on your own as an independent trainer, having credentials on your résumé will make a favorable impression on potential clients.

difficult people. Sometimes an employer will identify a key weakness in an employee and, rather than transferring, demoting, or firing her or him, the employer will hire a trainer to teach the employee how to delegate or how to network or whatever key skill he or she lacks in the position.

The theme of building trust and teamwork is another area where trainers are often employed. Many workplaces need to rely on unconventional incentives to sustain employee loyalty and collaboration when longevity and benefits are shrinking. In professions where groups of employees must rely on their colleagues, such as surgical teams, bringing in a trainer to conduct team-building exercises with the group has become almost standard. These sessions can be held in-house or take place in a camp-like or retreat setting. Trainers can also be hired to teach employees how to use computer software that is proprietary and required to do their jobs. Computer software training is one of the largest areas of corporate consulting, and it is likely to remain a growing field since general computer skills that employees may be expected to have when they are hired will not necessarily translate to being able to use specific software that is in place for a particular company. The growing field of customer service has also generated demand for trainers who teach representatives how to handle customer service calls.

The range of skills taught by a trainer in the nonprofit and government sectors covers the same ground as corporate trainers, with the addition that certain types of skills are more prevalent in these fields. Managing volunteers, for example, as well as effective community organizing, grant writing, and nonprofit-specific leadership skills are areas of training unique to nonprofits. Seminars on understanding public policy

Essential Gear

Pack your steamer trunk with business cards. The key to getting any kind of freelance work, whether you are a corporate trainer or a carpenter, is networking. Someone who has seen you work successfully as a grant writer or public speaker or team leader is more likely to hire you to train his or her employees in these subjects than a stranger. Word of mouth and reputation will help you, and so will some nice business cards and a sophisticated Web site. If you plan to teach training courses, videos of yourself teaching, brochures, or course outlines will also be useful for promotional purposes.

changes and laws are offered in the corporate sector, but they are particularly important for nonprofits and government agencies. Likewise, while public speaking is a skill required in certain areas of the private sector, it is even more in demand in the nonprofit and government sectors.

It should be apparent by now that what you can teach as a trainer largely depends on your skills and professional experience. Most trainers work closely with, and often have a background in, human resources.

Look to your present field for future prospects. Training is a natural outgrowth of hiring; and, indeed, some types of trainers teach interviewing skills, while others work closely with HR personnel to assess potential employees. Though anyone can hang out a shingle and offer their services as a trainer, getting work with a training company will require at least a bachelor's degree. An advanced degree in management or a related field will be required for some types of jobs, and specific certifications and degrees in training will be necessary as well. Some trainers simply come from a long career to instruct in their former specialties. A grant writer, for example, may change careers from writing grants to teaching others how to do so. A trainer in volunteer management for nonprofits likely spent a considerable amount of time managing volunteers him- or herself. In the field of fitness, some organizations may hire Spanish tutors for employees or meditation experts or yoga teachers, or even ergonomic consultants to help with workplace posture and habits. Some may bring in dicticians or lifestyle coaches to teach skills for balancing work and life. Your current field may be ripe for contract training work—whether you teach from it, teaching its principles to others, or to it, instructing people in the field how to maximize their performance.

The availability of consulting jobs, in "softer" skills areas especially, is closely tied to the health of the overall economy. In tough times, companies are most likely to cut their budgets for training that does not directly have an impact on their bottom line. When seas are rough, it is the extraneous cargo that will be thrown overboard, not the rum. So, the more critical the skill you teach, the more likely you are to be in demand. A company cannot forgo training on its proprietary software, making software training one of the safer areas of consulting. Your ability to combine consulting with a backup line of work is good assurance of a steady income.

You Are Here

You can begin your journey to training from many different locales.

Could you teach what you do now? Not all trainers teach a skill from a former career; some have specialized in corporate training itself since college. But an ideal way to transition into training from your current career is to find out if your current skill set is in demand by nonprofits and governments. Are you excellent at research but have not taught it? Substantiate your experience. Legitimize it by obtaining ready credentials if there are short courses you can take to certify your existing abilities. Having concrete work experience and coursework in your training area will give you credibility with clients. If you are teaching grant writing, for example, and can point to a track record of obtaining grants, you will find it easier to build a client base and gain the trust of your trainees. You can also draw upon your experience to answer a wide variety of queries from your trainees, and to formulate exercises and examples that accurately model real-world scenarios.

Navigating the Terrain

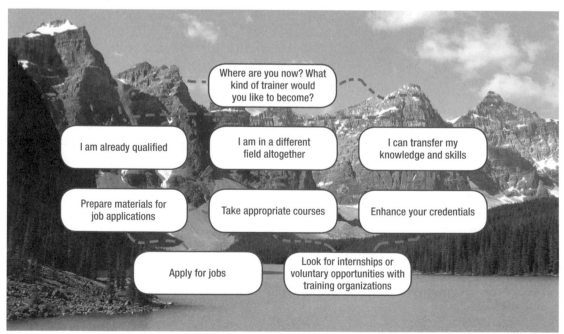

Do you have any teaching experience? As a trainer, you may work one-on-one with certain clients, especially if you are coaching a high-level manager, but much corporate training takes place in a typical classroom setting. You will be in front of a class like a regular teacher, so any teaching experience you have will benefit you on your new career path. The communication and organizational skills you needed for teaching will also be helpful, although you will not be grading your clients as you did your students. Performance experience is also useful, as you are "on" when in front of a class in much the same way as for a stage performance. Either teaching or performance experience will help to calm your nerves and make a good impression on potential employers when you are getting started and are new at training.

Do you have connections in the field? If you plan to work for a training company, it will most likely have a client base and send you out on assignments as a contractor. Larger companies will have a dedicated sales and marketing department that will secure clients for the trainers, but most training companies are smaller, often just a few trainers who have banded together to offer their services under one banner. You may also choose to work independently. In either case, you will need to drum up your own business. Connections in the nonprofit and public sectors will be invaluable. It is much easier to get hired by someone you know than to cold-call potential clients.

Organizing Your Expedition

Before you set out, know where you are going.

Decide on a destination. As you have seen in this chapter, there are many types of trainers working in a multitude of work environments. One advantage to being an independent contractor is that you get to experience a variety of workplaces. But this flexibility comes at the price of job security, stability, and benefits. You may finish an assignment not knowing when your next one will begin; therefore, it is important to frankly assess your financial needs as you decide which type of trainer to become. Do you have the connections to build a strong client base from the outset, or would you like the support of working for a large training company?

Notes from the Field

Judi Fleming
Training specialist, Transportation Security Administration (TSA)
Summerfield, North Carolina

What were you doing before you decided to change careers?

My undergraduate degree is in education and I started out as a high school teacher. When I wanted to leave high school teaching, I first changed careers into Web designer, and then worked as a software trainer for university faculty, staff, and students at the university where I was attending graduate school.

Why did you change your career?

I wanted to keep teaching, but in a different environment. I found myself gravitating towards teaching educational media. I liked the idea of teaching something technical, and teaching adults in a workplace

Are you prepared to market your services aggressively on your own, or would you prefer that someone else scare up the business and you just step in to do the actual training? Would you like a long-term assignment at one organization, or is moving around from jobsite to jobsite part of the appeal? Would you like your clients to come to you, such as at a retreat site, or are you willing to go to them? How much travel is appropriate and desirable for your family circumstances? Give some thought to these questions as you focus in on your destination.

Scout the terrain. Beginning with the Further Resources listed at the end of this chapter, join a professional organization for trainers in general or for your particular type, and look at job listings to determine the qualifications that you will need. Even if you are not certain that you want to work for a large training company, it does not hurt to schedule an informational interview to assess your compatibility with the company and discover part of how you are perceived in the marketplace, including learning what additional skills, experience, or certification would enhance your appeal. Software training in particular usually requires very specific certifications.

environment. I also saw that this was a field with flexibility and growth. Technology isn't going to go away, and it is only going to become more important that employees can use it effectively.

How did you make the transition?

I had just finished an MSEd degree in educational media and instructional design and went out on to what I thought was a "practice" interview. They offered me a job; I took it. I've been working for the government for over a decade now.

What are the keys to success in your new career?

When you work for the government, there is only one key to success: following government rules—no matter how silly, stupid or ludicrous you think they are.

Find the path that's right for you. Start by making an honest assessment of your financial needs. A trainer is a freelance consultant, an independent contractor who usually has no guarantee of another job when the current one ends. You may need to juggle marketing yourself with doing the actual training, which can be a difficult balance to strike on your own. You will be unlikely to have benefits or paid vacation time, and scheduling jobs to suit your clients will be paramount for building a good reputation in the business. If you need a degree or certification for your type of consulting, you need to consider what type of certification course is within your budget and schedule. Can you afford to go back to school full-time to acquire an additional degree? Is frequent travel a realistic option for you? Do you need health insurance? Can you afford to live on part-time wages while you are starting out and building your client base? The answers to these questions will help you set out on the right path.

Go back to school. Training is a line of work that is keyed to the experiences and personal strengths of the trainer. If your background is so far removed from your proposed training field that you would need to go back to school for a degree, you might want to consider whether training is the right field for you or, at least, whether you could train in an area that more closely fits your existing skill set. That said, master's degrees in public policy, nonprofit management, and related fields, can be a huge asset in substantiating your credentials as a trainer.

Landmarks

If you are in your twenties . . . You have some distinct advantages and disadvantages. One clear advantage is that you are more likely to still be in school or have the flexibility to return to school and obtain formal credentials in your training field. This formal schooling will help you get work as a trainer. Your main disadvantage is going to be lack of experience. No forty-plus executive is going to employ a twenty-something to teach him leadership skills or how to delegate. Your best bet may be to go into a high tech training area since everyone expects young people to be the computer experts; but if you are a whiz in another field and have charm almost to match, play to your strength.

If you are in your thirties or forties . . . You are at an ideal age to make a career transition into training. You are likely to have completed school and to have enough experience in your field to give you credibility teaching it. In certain fields, you might be able to begin training as a sideline, getting your feet wet and diving in full-time if opportunity and interest coincide. If you are a successful entrepreneur, for example, you might offer training workshops for prospective business owners through a local adult education center. If you are a grant writer for a nonprofit, you might teach a grant-writing course in the evenings.

If you are in your fifties . . . You have enough work experience behind you to give you substantial credibility as a trainer. You also may be ready for a big change in your life. If the kids are grown and the mortgage is paid-off, why not see what it is like to travel to different nonprofits or government agencies as a trainer? Before you embark, it is important to be aware that training is a risky field. In tough economic times, it will be one of the first expenses cut. Many organizations consider it a luxury and a perk for their employees. Transferring from a full-time career, especially a lucrative one, to starting out as a trainer can be unsettling if you are not prepared for it financially. Ask yourself if the financial resources you will need for the future, such as pensions, retirement funds, and health insurance, are in place before you disembark from your current job.

If you are over sixty . . . You may be eligible for retirement, but rather than heading into the sunset you feel ready to try a road less traveled. Since training jobs are often part-time and on short-term contracts, you are likely to face less discrimination than you would starting out at this age in many other fields. You also have a depth, and perhaps a breadth, of career experience that will keep you in demand for your expertise.

Further Resources

American Society for Training and Development is the main professional membership organization for workforce learning professionals, or trainers. http://www.astd.org

Alliance Training and Consulting, Inc. is a large training company with government and private sector contracts. Their Web site gives a good overview of the types of services that trainers offer and provides a useful example of how a large training company is organized. http://www.alliancetac.com

Langevin Learning Services is a company that trains trainers, providing workshops, certification programs, and extensive resources for new trainers. http://www.langevinonline.com

Everyone Ready is an online consulting company that trains volunteer leaders in the nonprofit sector. They have a large roster of experienced trainers, so looking at this site will give you an idea of what trainers do, how they do it, and the kinds of backgrounds that they have. http://www.energizeinc.com/everyoneready/index.html

Project Manager

Project Manager

Career Compasses

Get your bearings on what it takes to be a successful project manger.

Relevant Knowledge of how to manage projects in your line of work (40%)

Organizational Skills to keep track of your projects, equipment, and personnel (20%)

Communication Skills to deal with your project team effectively (30%)

Ability to Manage Stress is useful when you have to meet deadlines and face unexpected setbacks (10%)

Destination: Project Manager

If you think you would like to become a project manager, it is imperative that you have a solid grasp of what project management really is and how it developed as a distinct profession. It is important to first distinguish project management from the field of management more generally. Projects are finite endeavors; they have a distinct beginning, middle, and end. Managers can oversee certain types of personnel, such as a line manager on an assembly line or an administrative services manager in a law firm, or they can oversee a certain type of work, such as a production or operations manager. These are all ongoing concerns, without commencement or completion dates or sunset provisions for their budgets and staff. A project manager is distinguished from these other types of managers by virtue of the nature of his or her work. Projects are discrete events that can involve phases and long time frames but they do at some point reach completion and new projects commence. The management techniques and skills needed for project management are distinct from those in other types of management, and they have different philosophical underpinnings. Consider how the goals of a project manager differ from other types of managers. A manager of an ongoing or repetitive task or service strives to see that it is performed consistently and efficiently, with quality control. A project manager will have project-specific goals and benchmarks that will change from project to project. The resources for an ongoing management function may change with budget cuts or company expansion, but they remain largely fixed. A project has a specific budget, a time frame in which all of the projects objectives must be met, and (one hopes) a well-defined scope that is consistent with the project's budget and timeframe. In the abstract, a project manager will consider the goals and objectives of the project in light of its resource constraints and apply the most effective organization of resources to achieve the goals. In a sense, a project is like a puzzle. Only when all of the separate pieces are fitted in correctly will the desired picture emerge. Except that a project manager is not simply positioning pre-cut pieces; rather, he or she is cutting them and deciding how they should fit together. Lessons from similar past projects may guide the process, but

Essential Gear

Do not forget to record memories of your journey. Project managers all started out as members of project teams before moving up to positions of greater leadership and responsibility. If you have ever worked on a project where a manager who had no experience doing any of the jobs performed by project team members came on board, you will immediately see the importance of remembering what projects feel like from the position of team member. Avoid "look out below!" syndrome by making sure that you never forget what you liked and disliked about your PMs and avoiding behaviors that you remember to be annoying and counterproductive. Project teams appreciate good leadership but chafe and rebel under poor guidance.

each project rests on its merits and begins with a fresh slate. To accomplish the allocation of resources that will fulfill a project's goals and objectives within its time frame, budget, equipment, personnel, and other recourse constraints, a project manager employs variety of project management theories.

Prior to World War II, project management was conducted largely on an ad hoc basis, with no formal schools of thought employed or principles of organization studied by project managers. Beginning in the 1950s, various project management models and techniques were developed within the defense, construction, and engineering industries that spread quickly to other work environments. We can date the development of modern project management to this era. In 1969, the Project Management Institute (PMI) was founded, and today this organization still disseminates standards and guidelines for project managers that are widely accepted and employed. In 1981, PMI published *A Guide to the Project Management Body of Knowledge*, which has been updated as new techniques for project planning, scheduling, cost estimating, and related components of project management have been developed and refined. Of course, once the cat is let out of the bag one cannot stuff it back in, and the spread of project management guidelines has led to continual innovation both inside and outside of academia. Project management has become an academic discipline of its own, and each industry also continuously develops innovative industry-specific standards and techniques. There are many approaches to project management contained in these techniques and the intrepid career changer will need to be familiar with the most current ones specific to your industry.

Project managers can have varying degrees of responsibility. Sometimes the goals and resources of a project are set by others and the project manager simply has to work within them insofar as it is feasible to do so. In other situations, the project manager is responsible for taking some of the information, such as goals and time frame, scope and quality, and calculating how much of other inputs, such as budget and personnel, are needed.

Before you move on to read about the practical side of obtaining a project management job, think carefully about how the duties of a project manager differ from those who fulfill specific project functions on the project team. This dynamic career reserves its greatest rewards for those who strike a fine balance between doing and managing.

You Are Here

You can begin your journey to project management from many different locales.

Could you manage what you do now? Project management is not usually a separate career track on its own. Project managers usually work their way up the bureaucratic food chain, with a management position the reward for years of work on project teams. If you have solid experience in your current job, you could be closer than you think to a career change into project management. Bear in mind that being good at your current job does not automatically translate into being a good project manager. The skill set to be a worker bee is different from the talents and expertise of the queen bee; however, unlike the queen bee's, project management skills can be learned. If you are good at your job and have worked well on project teams thus far, you are well-positioned to explore a career move into project management.

Do you have any management experience or coursework? The skill set for management is quite specific. In much the same way that a good salesperson can sell anything, a good project manager can manage any project, within reason. Obviously, depending upon the industry, there are variables affecting the realistic delivery of the project that only someone experienced in the individual tasks that make up the project could know. Setting a timetable and other aspects of project management require some familiarity with the processes involved. But that does not stop organizations in the private, public, and nonprofit sectors from hiring management graduates or managers from other industries to come in at a senior level and oversee project team members.

Do you have excellent communication skills? A manager brought in from outside can encounter resistance and resentment if project team members perceive him or her to lack industry-specific knowledge and to be applying generic management techniques learned in school. Even if a manager is experienced in the industry, he or she can still encounter hostility if team members perceive that an outside hire was brought in rather than promote a senior member from the team. Finally, there is no guarantee of a smooth transition for the project team member who is

Navigating the Terrain

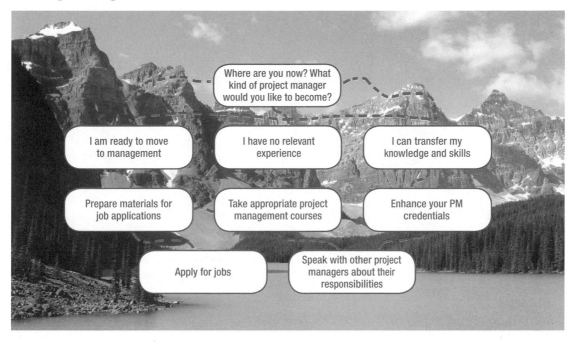

Where are you now? What kind of project manager would you like to become?

I am ready to move to management

I have no relevant experience

I can transfer my knowledge and skills

Prepare materials for job applications

Take appropriate project management courses

Enhance your PM credentials

Apply for jobs

Speak with other project managers about their responsibilities

promoted to oversee his or her former team members. In all three scenarios, solid communication skills can go a long way to earning respect and salving egos.

Organizing Your Expedition

Before you set out, know where you are going.

Decide on a destination. As you have read, project managers are usually senior employees in their field, who have worked their way up the hierarchy from junior to senior team member and then been promoted into a leadership role. So, if you are seeking a project management position in your current field, your first move is to find out the qualifications necessary to get a promotion at your existing job. Such a move is not a career change per se, except in the sense that the work of a project manager is quite different from the work of individual team members. It involves more oversight than hands-on participation in a project, and more people skills than

Notes from the Field
Gene Alexander
Environmental engineer/project manager
Chicago, Illinois

What were you doing before you decided to change careers?

Becoming a project manager was actually more of a promotion within my organization than a career change. Before becoming a project manager, I was an environmental engineer and member of project teams that provided technical support to project managers. The support I provided was primarily in planning and execution, while paying attention to factors that could contribute to technical or schedule risk, or that could otherwise compromise project execution.

Why did you change your career?

I view becoming a project manager as more of a transition to a position of greater responsibility within my career as an environmental engineer. In the process of career development, one's technical skills become refined over time, after which development into a management role would be expected of those who are competent. My motivations to advance are similar to most: The pursuit of new challenges and the higher pay that comes with having greater responsibility and personal accountability.

technical expertise. Some people find that they do not like the change, and discover that the only way out is down. To avoid that position, spend some time engaging in informational interviews with project managers to get a sense of their day-to-day duties. Ask yourself what you like about your current job and what you are eager to change or leave behind. Is one of your motivations to enter project management a lack of good leadership on the part of managers under which you have worked? That frustration may be a powerful impetus, but it does not in itself mean that you will like project management work. Likewise, disgust with bad management does not automatically imply that you will be a good manager. The skill set is different, and an honest assessment of your abilities and interests now will help you to an appropriate and satisfying career move in the near future.

How did you make the transition?

As an environmental engineer providing technical support to a project manager, I was involved in the planning, execution, and closing of projects. While providing technical support, I was mentored by various project managers as part of a succession management process within the organization. Over a period of about three years, I was increasingly exposed to and participated in the management aspects of a project, as well as receiving formal training and certification in project and contract management. When I was considered to be prepared, my management gave me project management assignments in addition to my technical support assignments. Then over a period of about two years my assignments shifted to being exclusively project management.

What are the keys to success in your new career?

I would say the keys to success as a project manager include awareness, adapting to uncertainty, and being committed to completing projects on time. It is critical to have a great project team supporting you, a team that is both technically competent and who can work well together. Projects need to be properly planned and adequately scoped out, with reasonable and attainable goals and milestones, along with recognition of potential risks that could interfere with execution or closure. With a good team supporting you, adversity can be dealt with and projects completed on time and within budget.

Scout the terrain. You may be queued and ready for a promotion in your field but there may be no openings at your current place of employment. That could change at any moment, but you will know if people in your desired position have a record of longevity and whether your employer is likely to be expanding or contracting in the foreseeable future. If you want to move up to management but do not see a way forward at your current place of employment, take a look at the many project management vacancies advertised online. Look for a headhunter in your field and send in your updated résumé. Make it known, discreetly, in your professional membership organizations that you are looking to move onward and upward. A little networking may land you the perfect job.

Find the path that's right for you. You may be feeling a bit left out because you want to enter project management but you are hoping to make a substantial career change and manage projects in a new field. While this is certainly possible, it is going to be slightly more difficult than simply climbing the hierarchy in your current industry. If you are determined to make this move, ask yourself why someone should hire you to manage projects in your desired area. What do you bring to the job that someone already working in that industry does not? If the answer is "project management experience," you may be able to make a semi-lateral move into a new career. You may also be able to make such a move if you have a management degree or coursework under your belt. But be aware that you will not have the respect of your project team members if you cannot perform any of their jobs.

Essential Gear

Pack your rucksack with leadership skills. Along the same lines as the above comment, do not assume that you can lead a project team just because you have been part of successful and well-coordinated teams in the past. Project leadership requires a different skill set than the one needed to do your specific task on the team. Read all you can about project management—there is no shortage of literature on the subject—so that you can get a handle on some of the skills that will be new to you in this role.

Go back to school. The number of undergraduate courses and graduate programs in management generally and project management specifically continues to grow at an alarming pace. You could easily go back to school for an MBA or other management degree and walk into a management position on the basis of the degree alone. Most universities and some colleges offer management courses. You can easily find the course offerings for schools in your area online. Today, it is usually possible to enroll for individual courses as a non-degree-seeking student, and management-related courses are often offered in the evenings to accommodate students' full-time work schedules.

Since project managers are often simply experienced workers in their field rather than specially trained managers (although this varies by industry), it can help you to have an advanced degree, or at least extensive coursework, in your discipline. In fact, it can be a condition of promotion for higher-level employees to have advanced degrees or certifications. Since this varies so much by industry, the best advice for you is to look at job advertisements for your desired project management position. Scrutinize the educational qualifications and see if you meet the minimum requirements. If not, you know what to do next. With some planning and preparation, your dream project management job can become a reality.

Landmarks

If you are in your twenties . . . You may be a bit young to take on a project management role in most industries. There are some exceptions, as the nonprofit sector, the entertainment industry, and the IT world sometimes provide opportunities for employees still in their twenties to take on positions of responsibility. Your wisest career move now is to learn all you can about your current job and conduct informational interviews with project managers in your field to find out what experience you need and what skills you need to develop to be eligible for promotion in a few years.

If you are in your thirties or forties . . . You are at the right age to ask about opportunities for promotion within your company. At your next review, mention to your boss that you are interested in moving up to a management role. If you are not scheduled for a performance review in the near future, make an appointment to speak with your boss or someone in human resources to make your case for a promotion. Plan carefully what you will say, making it clear that you want to move up because you enjoy where you work and you are not planning to leave. Be prepared for some honest feedback on what you need to do to be promotion-worthy, and work on areas that are suggested for improvement.

If you are in your fifties . . . You should have been tapped for a leadership role by now, unless you have changed careers already and lack sufficient experience. If you have been denied promotions, have a frank discussion with your boss about what qualities he or she thinks that you lack. Develop a plan to address any lacunae in your knowledge and skills and keep your employer abreast of your progress.

If you are over sixty . . . You should be able to draw on your previous professional experience to move up to a management role in your current job. If you have not been in line for a promotion to management after a long career in the same field, ask yourself why. Have you put yourself in line, made it known that you want to move up? If not, do so now, and prepare to stand convincingly against any age bias.

Further Resources

Project Management.com is a Web site devoted to project managers in the IT, construction and finance industries. It contains links to articles on best practices as well as abundant other resources. http://www.astd.org

Management Help.org is a site that contains resources for all aspects of management. It has extensive resources for project management. http://managementhelp.org/plan_dec/project/project.htm

Best Practices in Project Management is a resource-rich site maintained by the Information Services and Technology Department at MIT. http://web.mit.edu/ist/pmm

Michael Greer's Project Management Resources are compiled in a convenient list for your use. Most resources are free, but there is some proprietary information that he charges a fee to access. http://www.michaelgreer.com

Communications Manager

Communications Manager

Career Compasses

Get your bearings on what it takes to be a successful communications manager.

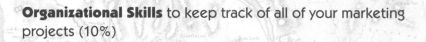

Relevant Knowledge of how to market your employer (30%)

Organizational Skills to keep track of all of your marketing projects (10%)

Ability to Manage Stress is a handy quality to possess when you are faced with big events like conferences or competing deadlines and priorities, not to mention difficult bosses or colleagues (10%)

Communication Skills would seem to be an obvious requirement for a communications manager (50%)

Destination: Communications Manager

If you are contemplating a career change into communications management, it is likely that you already have some familiarity with the functions and duties of this profession. Nonetheless, it is worth discussing them briefly to clarify the role for any readers who are curious but not certain about this dynamic career option. In a nutshell, a communications manager markets his or her employer's work by preparing brochures, hosting events, issuing press releases, and generating other marketing materials as appropriate. Marketing is the typical degree and professional background of communications managers, but transferring from both related fields, such as advertising and sales, and unrelated fields, is possible.

After reading the above, you might wonder: Are communications managers marketers or advertisers, and what is the difference? It is easy to confuse marketing and advertising and many people use the terms interchangeably. In fact, advertising is a form of marketing. Advertising involves placing paid ads for your employer's products or services in various media, including direct mail, billboards, television, radio, the Internet, and print media such as newspapers and magazines. Marketers use advertising as one strategy of promotion, but it is not the only tool in their arsenal. Some marketers may spend a lot of time, effort, and money on advertising, but others may focus more on other aspects of promotion, such as market research, media planning, public relations, product pricing, distribution, customer support, sales strategy, and community involvement. Therefore, communications managers will often use advertising, but the job entails much more than ad development and placement. The terms marketing and advertising are usually associated with the private sector. A company that sells widgets will have a sales and marketing department whose staff uses advertising, market research, and other strategies to sell things. This team will typically be led by a director of marketing who oversees a marketing manager or several and various layers of hierarchy in the department. Some duties, such as conducting polls or writing commercials or other ad copy and art may be outsourced but overseen by the department.

In the public and nonprofit sectors, the person in the role of director of marketing or marketing manager is usually known as a communications manager. The job duties are similar but the different terminology reflects the important distinction between marketing a consumer product or service and marketing something less tangible, such as education or poverty eradication or another charitable cause. In other words, the marketing director for a tuna company is trying to persuade you to buy cans of tuna at the grocery store, whereas the communications manager for Save the Whales is trying to persuade you to make a financial contribution toward a campaign to preserve ocean habitat on the other side of the world. The latter is clearly less tangible a commodity, and the motivations for the targeted consumer are different in each case—a fact which lends itself to different marketing strategies for each type of campaign. Someone working in marketing in the private sector could make this career change easily, but it is worth keeping aware of this key difference between commercial and nonprofit marketing.

Because the nonprofit sector relies heavily on name recognition and reputation to secure contributions, the public relations aspect of this job is crucial. Public relations is technically a separate activity from media relations, yet the main way that an organization reaches the public these days is via the media, causing these two job duties to overlap and merge significantly. A campaign manager with a large budget and staff will not be writing press releases and developing media and public relations strategies alone. Rather, he or she will work with a public relations agency that specializes in this function. Likewise, a communications manager may contract with a polling organization to conduct polls to gauge public perception of the organization and its activities.

Another distinctive feature of marketing in the nonprofit sector is the use of moral suasion rather than cold hard cash to garner media attention and engage in PR. You may not have the advertising budget of a private sector company as your employer does not turn a profit from your work. Persuading local media to report on your efforts and notify the public of upcoming events is an important part of a communications manager's job. Nonprofits frequently run advertisements known as PSAs (public service announcements). These advertisements are designed to disseminate important information to the public rather than to sell a product to potential consumers. Many of the same strategies and tactics that are used in public sector marketing work in the nonprofit sector but

Essential Gear

Take your creativity along for the ride. Have you ever seen a marketing ploy, such as an advertisement, and thought, "Wow, that is really clever!" A classic example is the famous Taco Bell newspaper advertisement on April Fool's Day 1993, with a picture of the Liberty Bell and the caption that the company had purchased it and it would henceforth be known as the "Taco Liberty Bell." No one who has ever seen that advertisement has forgotten it, and most still chuckle at the memory. Someone in the company's marketing department was thinking creatively. In your work as a communications manager, you will not be selling a product, you will be selling your organization's work and mission. You, too, will need to think creatively to capture the public's attention.

the tone is usually noticeably different. There is an art to framing a message for public consumption. Effective marketing is a talent as well as a learned skill.

Another activity that will occupy your time and energies as a communications manager is event planning. Nonprofit organizations hold many types of events to promote their work and fundraise. An animal rescue group, for example, may hold adoption days where animals appear on local television and mobile adoption units are set up in a well-traveled public area. They might also hold fundraising dinners, raffle nights, fundraising events such as car or dog washes, auctions, and conferences and seminars. Some events may be small and informal, whereas others may be black-tie affairs populated by Hollywood stars and paparazzi. For an example of a nonprofit organization that uses a wide variety of marketing strategies and holds several prominent fundraising and public education events per year, check out http://www.bestfriends.org. As you can see from its Web site, Best Friends is an animal rescue based in Utah. Its PR apparatus is large and sophisticated, so it provides an excellent demonstration of the work of a communications manager. This is, of course, only one example. If you receive materials regularly from your alma mater, those brochures and invites, calendars and surveys are the work of a communications manager and his or her staff. Think you could do a better job? Perhaps you are right. Give it a try and see where this exciting career path leads.

Do PR campaigns and event planning sound like your speed? Is there an organization or cause whose work you think you could promote effectively? If so, read on for more on taking a dive into the rapidly moving waters of communications management.

You Are Here

You can begin your journey to communications management from many different locales.

Have you had any advertising experience? Yes, we made it clear that advertising is only one small piece of the work of a communications manager, but it is an important piece. Even if all you have worked on is a fake advertising campaign for a class project, mention it among your credentials. Many potential contributors in the nonprofit world are put off by the guilt-inducing tone of many advertisements that solicit funds or demonstrate a lack of goods and services for the poor. Make your work positive and hopeful and you will attract employers as well as reach the public effectively.

Do you work in marketing already? As noted above, this is really a marketing job, and any marketing experience that you have will make the transition smoother. If you currently have a private sector marketing job and long to make the switch to communications management, start by looking for jobs on http://www.idealist.org. On your résumé, play up your marketing experience, and on your cover letter, make it abundantly clear why you want to work for that particular nonprofit. If your passion is convincing, your experience will pave the way for you to land your dream job.

Essential Gear

Pack your suitcase with written work. A communications manager does a lot of highly focused writing that must show off the key aspects of their organization or program in the best light, targeted to specific audiences such as donors or the public. Writing for public relations is a learned skill and potential employers will want to see that you have acquired it before they hire you. If you are moving into this career from another field, it is particularly important that you demonstrate your ability to write effectively. Take your best writing examples and compile them into a portfolio that you can submit with job applications to impress potential employers and show them that you possess this vital communications skill.

Do you have a relevant degree? Even if you are switching from a completely different line of work, you may have taken some classes in college or graduate school that may be worth highlighting on your résumé or in your cover letter. Did you major in communications, marketing, advertising, public relations, media relations, or nonprofit or public sector management? How about journalism or English? Did you do a lot of writing? Do you have any awards for your writing or previous freelance writing work? If you cast your mind back to your school days, whether they were a few months or a few decades ago, look at your educational background with a fresh perspective, geared toward your new career goal, and highlight anything that may be of value on the job market. Play it up in your applications. It cannot hurt, and it certainly may help.

Navigating the Terrain

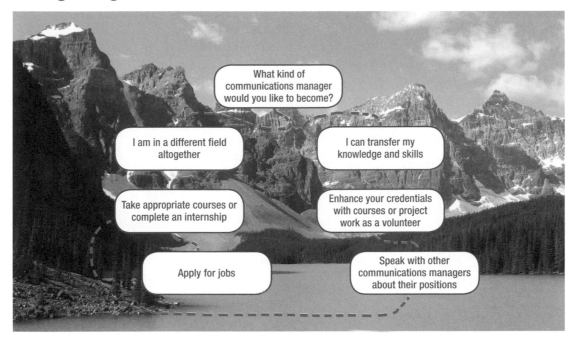

What kind of communications manager would you like to become?

I am in a different field altogether

I can transfer my knowledge and skills

Take appropriate courses or complete an internship

Enhance your credentials with courses or project work as a volunteer

Apply for jobs

Speak with other communications managers about their positions

Organizing Your Expedition

Before you set out, know where you are going.

Decide on a destination. It should be clear by now that communications managers work in a wide variety of organizations. They work for the government, in federal agencies, and state bureaucracy too. They work extensively in the nonprofit sector, and they also play an important role in academia. Communications managers are critical to getting the word out about the research being conducted in academic departments at colleges and universities. They help to attract students and faculty, to bolster the reputation of the school, and, most importantly, to appeal to donors. Where would you like to work? Are you driven by the mission of one type of organization, or does the work itself interest you and you could market anything? Many salespeople say that they can sell anything, it does not matter what it is; it is simply in their blood to be able to sell effectively. If you feel that way about communications management,

Notes from the Field

Eliana Smith
Communications manager
Albuquerque, New Mexico

What were you doing before you decided to change careers?

I had several positions as publicity director in publishing and in higher education. I had a Ph.D. in English, and I taught at several colleges after I received my doctorate.

Why did you change your career?

I found that publicity was too focused on making that next pitch and I wanted a position that offered a range of communications activities, including writing, publications, and project management. Before I moved into publishing, I had already decided that academia was not for me.

How did you make the transition?

I did lots of informational interviewing to learn what I needed to add to my résumé. I asked each person for their advice about what I should do to prepare myself for the change—people love to talk about what they know—and soon I developed a fairly comprehensive understanding of the market and what I needed to do to enter it. For example, I

then your job prospects are wide indeed. If you have a more specific goal, such as working for a human rights nonprofit or a children's medical nonprofit, you may have to be more geographically flexible to find the right job for you.

Scout the terrain. Your first move should be to take stock of your local prospects. Are there research universities in the vicinity? How about headquarters of major charitable organizations? If you live in a major city, particularly one on the East Coast, you may find many job opportunities close to home. If you live farther afield, do not despair. There are colleges and universities scattered all over the country, some in very out-of-the-way rural locations, and they all employ communications managers. Nonprofits can also be based out of unexpected places, and do not learned that I needed a more varied portfolio of articles, so I sought out freelance opportunities to write news and feature articles. I followed up on every lead and found that people really appreciate it when you are diligent—they can't always offer you a job, but they usually can give you a really useful piece of advice, throw a freelance assignment your way, or give you a tip about when a job might open up. In part because of my lack of experience, my first transition required a pay cut, but the new position had lots of room for growth and was an excellent fit.

What are the keys to success in your new career?

A communications manager is in charge of many different kinds of projects, so I would say that the most important qualities are flexibility, the ability to pay attention to details without losing sight of the big picture, and excellent organizational skills to ensure that all deadlines are met on projects no matter how large and small. It's also important to remember that communications is a service position—building good relationships will always benefit you, so you must work on building relationships continually. Going the extra mile for others is a critical aspect of your work. Listen carefully to both the letter and the spirit of what people want in a project so that you are able to deliver the most effective product.

forget the option of telecommuting. This is a growing method of working in this field, and you should feel free to ask a potential employer about the possibility of telecommuting even if it is not mentioned in the job announcement.

Find the path that's right for you. One of the best ways to find the right job fit and to make this career transition a success is to seek out informational interviews. Write to the communications managers and human resources personnel of organizations where you would like to work and request an informational interview. Dress as you would for a regular job interview, bring copies of your résumé and samples of related work, and be prepared to ask focused questions. Come with a list and ask about the day-to-day job duties of someone in your desired role, as well as the necessary qualifications. Ask communications managers what courses they took in school and how they landed their first jobs. Follow up with a thank you note and leave a copy of your résumé. If you can swing an internship, ask about any opportunities they may have, but do not be too pushy about looking for a job from an informational interview. Politeness and tact will go a long way toward making a good impression.

Go back to school. The question of going back to school before making a career change into this field is tricky. On the one hand, there are specific degrees and courses that are particularly well-suited to communications management, such as communications (obviously), marketing, advertising, public relations, media relations, and general business or nonprofit management. On the other hand, a high percentage of people employed in this field have moved into it without the prescribed educational background and have done quite well. Experience in writing, fundraising, project management, nonprofit or public sector management, and many other fields, including teaching, have provided an adequate springboard for launching a career in communications. If you find that your experience is too far removed to make the switch, consider taking individual courses in communications or public relations rather than going back to school for another degree, which might not be necessary. You will need to apply for jobs and play it by ear.

Landmarks

If you are in your twenties . . . Your strategy to market yourself as a communications director involves majoring in communications, if you are still in school, or at least taking courses in this or a related field such as marketing, advertising, public relations, or media relations. The other phase of your career change plan involves getting an internship. This will give you valuable experience and could lead to a job offer.

If you are in your thirties or forties . . . You may have established yourself in another field, and the key question to ask yourself is: what are your transferable skills? You will need to demonstrate to potential employers why they should choose you over candidates who are experienced in this field already. Your first marketing job will be selling yourself. If you have

any connections in organizations that appeal to you, see if you can get hired on a project basis to prove your mettle.

If you are in your fifties . . . You have several options that depend upon how closely related your previous experience is. What communications manager skills do you already possess? What skills do you need? Look at job advertisements and see where the holes are in your qualifications. Bear in mind that you may need to take a pay cut to move into this job if you are in a senior position in another field.

If you are over sixty . . . You can look to the advice for fifty-somethings, above, as well as considering some creative ways of entering the field that are open to you if you have another source of income, such as retirement savings or a pension. It may be tough to get an internship since they are usually geared toward neophyte workers, but you could volunteer to work on some projects to both gain skills and demonstrate how you could be an asset to your proposed employer.

Further Resources

Public Relations Society of America (PRSA) is the world's largest membership organization of public relations professionals. Web site includes a job center. http://www.prsa.org

Communication Service Public Relations Council is a nonprofit organization for communications management professionals in community service agencies that provides information on public relations and fundraising to its members. http://stlouis.missouri.org/501c/csprc/index.html

Center for Giving has published a useful article called "Communication and Marketing Resources for the Nonprofit Sector." http://www.centerforgiving.org/s_map/bin.asp?cid=4449&did=12350&doc=file.pdf

The NonProfit Times is an online newspaper for the nonprofit world. It is published biweekly and includes job listing for positions such as communications manager. http://www.nptimes.com

Public Official- - - -

Public Official

Career Compasses

Get your bearings on what it takes to be a successful public official.

Relevant Knowledge of the needs and policy preferences of your constituents (30%)

Organizational Skills to manage your campaign finances, staff, issues, and other matters (20%)

Communication Skills are absolutely essential for reaching out to voters (20%)

Caring about your constituents and their problems is a good quality for a public official to possess (30%)

Destination: Public Official

This is the ideal career change for this series because anyone, from virtually any walk of life, regardless of educational or professional or family background, can run for public office. If you are a U.S. citizen, you can serve your country and your fellow citizens in some capacity as a public official. There are many public offices, at the local, state, and national levels, from which to choose; all you need to do is research which is a good match for your needs and interests. Then you need to get elected or appointed—that is the tricky part. But it is doable if you have the drive, ambition, and ability to compromise that are the necessary attributes of a public official.

The first step on the journey to entering public service is asking yourself what motivates you to enter this field. Except for top officials who earn six-figure salaries, the public sector is not as lucrative as the private, although former public officials can often command high salaries when they go back on the job market due to their connections and experience. There is a fame element to public service, but it certainly is not as glamorous as other careers that get your name and picture in the news. Some people enter public service because they come from a family that has a tradition of running for office, serving in the military, or other connections to the public sector. The initial motivation for many people entering government work is prestige. It is a good feeling to receive mail addressed to "The Honorable [Your Name Here]" and to walk in the footsteps of our forefathers in shaping, executing, and enforcing the laws of the country. But by far the chief motivating factor for seeking public office is power. The lure of power provides the initial impetus to run and the obtainment and wielding of power feeds ambition to seek more power as oxygen feeds a fire. There are a few people who enter public service motivated by the desire to make concrete change in some policy area, such as education, energy, health care, or poverty, about which they have passionate views. Policy-oriented ambitions are not usually sufficient to withstand one campaign, let alone tenure in any public post. It may sound cynical, but it is the honest truth that no altruistic motives can withstand the frustration of actual government service. The idealism will be knocked out of you and, the higher office you seek, the

Essential Gear

Take a poll. In fact, take several polls. Candidates for public office rely on public opinion polls to gauge voter receptivity to their campaign. Is your name known? You cannot win if voters are unfamiliar with you. What do voters think of your stand on issues that are relevant to them? Where do your potential constituents stand on these issues? Polls are a useful mechanism for fundraising because potential donors like to fund a winner. If you are doing well in the polls, this will attract donations to your campaign.

more you will have to compromise your principles to get there. We lament the chameleon-like nature and lack of principles of our politicians but we must acknowledge that it is the system that makes them that way. Ideological purity is not useful in the environment of practical compromise that characterizes pluralist politics.

Now that you have given some thought to your motivation for entering public service, the next step is to set your sights on an obtainable initial post. As explained in more detail later in the chapter, your best bet is to start with a local position and work your way up. Many politicians begin their careers by running for the local school board. Running for local office will give you a taste of public life, with its endless cycle of fundraising and campaigning, so you will be able to assess whether you are suited to this lifestyle. It takes a certain personality type to blossom in the public eye. You need to be able to talk to people from all walks of life and make them feel that you know their problems and priorities and that you can relate to them personally. Former president Bill Clinton excelled at this skill, as do many successful politicians. You need to be comfortable making eye contact, shaking a lot of hands, and it helps tremendously to have a good head for names. In order to select you to represent them, voters need to feel that you know and understand them. The ability to convey empathy is crucial, and its lack has been the downfall of many an otherwise qualified candidate. We often laugh when we see a candidate who appears to be making a fool of him- or herself as an obvious fish out of water in some campaign stop (think Hillary Rodham Clinton on a bar stool wearing a John Deere cap and downing shots), but these charades are necessary to build the illusion of empathy with voters. Even if you are a teetotaling, vegetarian pacifist who has never held a gun, you are going to need to put on some blaze orange and sling a rifle over your shoulder while having a beer with the local hunters to gain their trust and its reward: their vote.

In addition to gaining the trust of voters, another secret to electoral success is running a disciplined and organized campaign. Fundraising is hard work, and you need to focus on spending that money where it will do you the most good. No politician works alone. Aside from family, behind every successful political candidate there is a skillful campaign manager running the show. Think the Wizard of Oz. The great and powerful wizard would have been nothing but a puff of smoke without the real mastermind behind the curtain. You, too, will need a hire a savvy campaign manager to help you strategize and to coordinate fundraising, media relations, and to manage volunteers. You probably will not be able to hire David Axelrod to manage your mayoral campaign, but do get the most politically savvy and well-connected campaign manager you can afford. Today, there are many political consulting firms that provide complete campaign management services, including fundraising, carrying out public opinion polls, and advising you on how to target your message. The amount that they charge varies, so do your research before you hire one.

Another item that you will need to mount a viable campaign is signage. Name recognition is half the battle, so you need to get your name out there. Signs, buttons, banners, bumper stickers, and other campaign paraphernalia are available from a variety of sources, depending upon your budget and needs. One source for all types of signage is Run and Win. There are many others, and it might pay off to patronize local businesses.

Last but not least, you will need volunteers to distribute information, conduct polls, answer questions from the media and the public, fundraise, stuff envelopes, and provide energy, enthusiasm, and support. In your first campaign, the volunteers will likely consist of your family, friends, neighbors, and colleagues. So be sure to stay on everyone's good side! In fact, that is good advice for political candidates in general. Read on for more detailed information on how to make a career change into public service.

You Are Here

You can begin your journey to government office from many different locales.

Is your life's journey thus far an open travel diary? That's a thematic way of asking if your life is the proverbial open book. It had better not be a surprise to you that virtually every detail of the private lives of candidates for public office, both elected and appointed, is scrutinized. If you are running for office, your opponent will dig up any embarrassing facts about your past that could cost you votes. If you are a potential nominee for an appointed position, the office of the official who has selected you for a post will require you to disclose anything that could potentially embarrass the official or your political party. For offices as low as a seat on the town council, you may be asked to sign a loyalty oath where you swear not to embarrass your party before they will seat you in your elected position. Higher-level government positions may require background checks that oblige you to disclose information about everyone with whom you have ever associated, as well as all of your financial records. Before taking office, then-president Barack Obama developed an infamous 63-question application for potential appointees asking for applicants' every past online alias or user name. Overall, it seems, colorful Internet living may keep many from the possibility of public service.

Is your family on board with your plans? As a public official, your life will change radically, and so will that of your family. If you hold a state or national office, you will mostly likely have to move to your state capital or Washington, D.C. Your children may have to change schools, and your spouse may have to change jobs. If you spouse's work presents a potential conflict of interest, you may have to decide whose career will take precedence. Your family will be expected to stump for you on the campaign trail, to submit to media interviews and scrutiny, and, in some cases, to live under increased security. Everyone in your family will have to be acutely conscious of how their actions could reflect on you, and the public facade of your family must always be of cheerful, smiling harmony. Your job may not come with a salary, but it might demand attendance at long meetings in the evenings, shifting extra familial duties to your spouse.

Do you know how you will fund your campaign? The higher the office, the more expensive the campaign, and each election cycle seems to break the spending records set at the previous one. Most candidates start with a local campaign that does not require extensive capitalization to be successful. In subsequent elections, if you move up to state or even national elected office, you will need to have a private source of funding, such as being independently wealthy, or be prepared and able to raise funds. If asking for money makes you uncomfortable, you might want to reconsider whether a political career is a viable option for you.

Navigating the Terrain

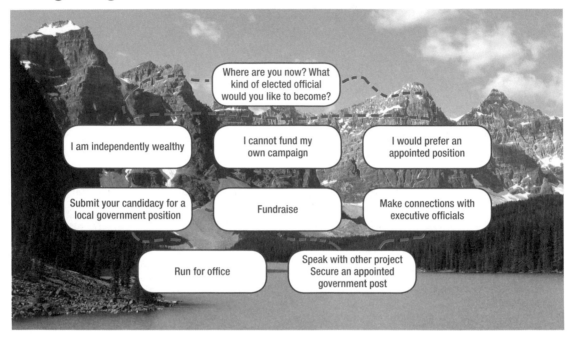

Where are you now? What kind of elected official would you like to become?

I am independently wealthy

I cannot fund my own campaign

I would prefer an appointed position

Submit your candidacy for a local government position

Fundraise

Make connections with executive officials

Run for office

Speak with other project Secure an appointed government post

Organizing Your Expedition

Before you set out, know where you are going.

Decide on a destination. Is your ultimate goal to be president of the United States? Perhaps you have more modest ambitions, such as to be mayor of your town or to become a judge in your county. Whether your goal is the White House or the town hall, your path is essentially the same: Start by getting involved in your local community. Volunteer, show up regularly for town meetings, become knowledgeable about local political issues, and get acquainted with the basis of the local economy. Eat out a lot. Seriously, this will help you get to know your neighbors. Get to know the owners of local businesses. Write letters to the local paper. The more well known you are in your community (for positive reasons), the better. Aside from party affiliation, most voters use name recognition as their main basis for making a selection in the voting booth.

Remember that reaching your ultimate goal involves a series of interim steps. If you want to be a Supreme Court judge, for example, you will need to go to law school, secure a prestigious clerkship with one of the nation's higher courts, get a top legal job and make a name for yourself as a prosecutor, law professor, or other prominent area of law. You might want to avoid becoming a criminal defense or personal injury lawyer if you are calculating what will look good in terms of future appointment prospects. Your next step would be to become a judge at the local or state level. Most states elect judges, but the systems for doing this are idiosyncratic and vary by state. Once you have gotten yourself elected to a state judgeship, you will need to establish a reputation that will put you in line for a federal appointment. All federal judges are nominated by the president and confirmed by the Senate. Judges usually start out in federal circuit courts and then, as vacancies arise, they may be nominated for the federal appeals court in their circuit. Only a rare few will have the opportunity to be elevated to the nation's highest court. Vacancies on the Supreme Court of the United States are few and far between. But there is no harm in dreaming big, just take the steps you need to put you in a position to take advantage of opportunities when they arise.

Essential Gear

Check qualification requirements carefully. Every public office, from a seat on the local school board to president of the United States, has specific qualifications that you must meet in order to run for that office. Most offices have residency and citizenship requirements. That is, you must be a U.S. citizen and you must have lived in your town, county, district, or state for a certain number of years prior to running for office. There are age requirements for many offices as well. Certain offices, like attorney general or surgeon general, will require that you have a law or medical degree and have passed the bar or medical boards. Before you run for any public office, look up its specific requirements and be sure that you qualify. And be sure that you are registered to vote in the locality where you propose to run for public office!

Scout the terrain. The above example is instructive whatever office you seek: Start small and local and work your way up, make sure you have the educational background and connections necessary to move up the food chain. Set your initial sights on an open seat; that is, a seat

Notes from the Field

Colleen Fisch
Supervisor #2, Town of Bristol
Bristol, Wisconsin

What were you doing before you decided to change careers?

I was working in medical product management and sales. I had enjoyed product management, which constantly involved learning new things, but I had made the mistake of switching to sales, which offered more opportunity financially but virtually no challenges.

Why did you change your career?

My job had gotten boring and lacked challenge on any level. . . . I knew that I was staying only because I did care about my manufacturers, suppliers, and customers and because I could do the job in my sleep.

How did you make the transition?

Since I was bored at work and only going there for the money, I began talking to my spouse about not working. We had already determined that it was time to start a family and I knew that if I possibly could, I would want to be at home when my children were young. At the same time I was attending town board and zoning meetings and developing serious concerns about the direction of our town government. It oc-

without an incumbent. It is difficult to win against an incumbent, even one who is not very popular. Occasionally, incumbents can be unseated, but it rarely happens due to the fact that their past victories have given them name recognition and fundraising abilities, not to mention other advantages that come with their office that help with reelection. If you really want a position for which there is not likely to be an open seat for the foreseeable future, go ahead and try. A campaign is good experience even if you lose. Many of today's highest officials have lost election bids in their pasts.

Find the path that's right for you. Campaigning for and serving in public office are both very demanding on your time, finances, and energies. It is also a lifestyle that can place tremendous strain on your family.

curred to me that I actually really cared about what happened in my area. When I learned I was pregnant, I made arrangements to leave my job. I ended up filing papers to run for office about two weeks later. Because I ended up miscarrying, I was able to campaign aggressively that spring and win a seat on our town board. There is some training offered for new board members, but it is such a lowly political position that you end up learning on the job. It does require a lot of work, but it is work from home for the most part, and it is work about which I care very much. It made sense to pursue the job because I was already invested in the community and it felt like a natural fit.

What are the keys to success in your new career?

There are quite a few, including meeting and listening to area residents; having, defining, and articulating a very clear vision and direction that I want to see the town go in; sharing the vision and creating synergy wherever I can; and last but certainly not least, continuing to meet with and listen to area residents to affirm that our goals remain mutual. I created and maintain a promotional town Web site and a community group. I continue to show up to make our vision heard whenever I can. Stepping up and showing up when so few others do is what makes the difference in our local governments.

Some lower-level government positions are unpaid, but carry a heavy workload that can conflict with your paid employment. If you can, talk to someone (not a potential rival) who is serving in your desired role and find out firsthand all you can about the job and how the officeholder balances work, family, and public service.

Go back to school. There are no specific degree requirements for the vast majority of public offices. There are a few positions, elected or appointed, that call for a law or medical degree, but you would not go through the time and expense of obtaining these degrees just for the remote possibility of gaining one of those positions. It is true that many public officials tend to be lawyers, but it is not a requirement. No master's or doctorate is required to hold public office, but a bachelor's is commonly held. Some local offices may be reachable without a college degree, but you would be wise to complete a bachelor's if you do not have one. The subject of your major is not important. Have you ever heard of a candidate's undergraduate major being a campaign issue? Majoring in political science, pre-law, economics, history, or communications are all common majors for students with political ambitions, but a drama degree seems to work equally well.

Landmarks

If you are in your twenties . . . Your age will work against you in some respects, and to your advantage in others. You are too young to be eligible for many public offices, and you will face resistance from older voters who will not trust someone so young to represent them in government. Yet you are in an ideal position to lay the groundwork for future campaigns. You can volunteer to work on political campaigns and learn the ropes of running a campaign, gaining expertise in essential skills like fundraising. There are also some offices that are open to you over the age of 21 or 25—check the specific requirements in your state and locality.

If you are in your thirties or forties . . . You may be ready to enter politics as a career. The key is to start small: Run for your local school or town board, learn how to fundraise and make connections, and then set your sights on a state-level office. From the state level, you can try to move on to national office as the opportunity arises. Your first public office may be an unpaid, part-time position that will accommodate your current job.

If you are in your fifties . . . You have sufficient life experience to lend gravity to your campaign. Play up your connections to your community and any community service that you have put in over the years. The more well known and invested you seem in your local area, the more you will endear yourself to voters. This is the time to press friends and family into volunteering their time and energies for your campaign, and to use every connection that you possess.

If you are over sixty . . . You can read the advice for the over-fifty set, above, and consider that it applies to you. If you are retired, you can make it a point in your campaign to emphasize that you have the time to devote to your new office. Make sure that you are photographed playing sports, running, cycling, or otherwise showing that you are youthful and energetic for your age. Make sure that your age is spun positively to show off your experience and that your opponents have no basis to claim that you would not have the energy or clarity of focus for the office.

Further Resources

Run for Office.org is a one-stop shop for information no how to run your first campaign. It includes information on eligibility requirements for various offices by state. http://www.runforoffice.org

League of Women Voters has a page with state-by-state contact information for election services. You can contact your state to find out what you need to do to file paperwork to run for office, and look up the requirements for each state position. http://www.lwv.org

Project Vote Smart has a list of political resources on its Web site that includes links to essential demographic information for anyone contemplating running for public office. There is plenty of other useful information on the site as well. http://www.votesmart.org/resource_political _resources.php?category=13

Campaign Window is a service that, for a small fee, will help you build a Web site for your campaign. Includes an interface for submitting campaign contributions and the ability to send email blasts. http://campaignwindow.com

Appendix A

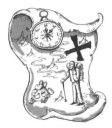

Going Solo: Starting Your Own Business

Starting your own business can be very rewarding—not only in terms of potential financial success, but also in the pleasure derived from building something from the ground up, contributing to the community, being your own boss, and feeling reasonably in control of your fate. However, business ownership carries its own obligations—both in terms of long hours of hard work and new financial and legal responsibilities. If you succeed in growing your business, your responsibilities only increase. Many new business owners come in expecting freedom only to find themselves chained tighter to their desks than ever before. Still, many business owners find greater satisfaction in their career paths than do workers employed by others.

The Internet has also changed the playing field for small business owners, making it easier than ever before to strike out on your own. While small mom-and-pop businesses such as hairdressers and grocery stores have always been part of the economic landscape, the Internet has made reaching and marketing to a niche easier and more profitable. This has made possible a boom in *microbusinesses*. Generally, a microbusiness is considered to have under ten employees. A microbusiness is also sometimes called a *SoHo* for "small office/home office."

The following appendix is intended to explain, in general terms, the steps in launching a small business, no matter whether it is selling your Web-design services or opening a pizzeria with business partners. It will also point out some of the things you will need to bear in mind. Remember also that the particular obligations of your municipality, state, province, or country may vary, and that this is by no means a substitute for doing your own legwork. Further suggested reading is listed at the end.

Crafting a Business Plan

It has often been said that success is 1 percent inspiration and 99 percent perspiration. However, the interface between the two can often be hard to achieve. The first step to taking your idea and making it reality is constructing a viable *business plan*. The purpose of a business plan is to think things all the way through, to make sure your ideas really are profitable, and to figure out the "who, what, when, where, why, and how" of your business. It fills in the details for three areas: your goals, why you think they are attainable, and how you plan to get to there. "You need to know where you're going before you take that first step," says Drew Curtis, successful Internet entrepreneur and founder of the popular newsfilter Fark.com.

Take care in writing your business plan. Generally, these documents contain several parts: An *executive summary* stating the essence of the plan; a *market summary* explaining how a need exists for the product and service you will supply and giving an idea of potential profitability by comparing your business to similar organizations; a *company description* which includes your products and services, why you think your organization will succeed, and any special advantages you have, as well as a description of *organization* and *management*; and your *marketing and sales strategy*. This last item should include market highlights and demographic information and trends that relate to your proposal. Also include a *funding request* for the amount of start-up capital you will need. This is supported by a section on *financials*, or the sort of cash flow you can expect, based on market analysis, projection, and comparison with existing companies. Other needed information, such as personal financial history, résumés, legal documents, or pictures of your product, can be placed in *appendices*.

Use your business plan to get an idea of how much startup money is necessary and to discipline your thinking and challenge your preconceived notions before you develop your cash flow. The business plan will tell you how long it will take before you turn a profit, which in turn is linked to how long it will before you will be able to pay back investors or a bank loan—which is something that anyone supplying you with money will want to know. Even if you are planning to subside on grants or you are not planning on investment or even starting a for-profit company, the discipline imposed by the business plan is still the first step to organizing your venture.

A business plan also gives you a realistic view of your personal financial obligations. How long can you afford to live without regular income? How are you going to afford medical insurance? When will your business begin turning a profit? How much of a profit? Will you need to reinvest your profits in the business, or can you begin living off of them? Proper planning is key to success in any venture.

A final note on business plans: Take into account realistic expected profit minus realistic costs. Many small business owners begin by underestimating start-ups and variable costs (such as electricity bills), and then underpricing their product. This effectively paints them into a corner from which it is hard to make a profit. Allow for realistic market conditions on both the supply and the demand side.

Partnering Up

You should think long and hard about the decision to go into business with a partner (or partners). Whereas other people can bring needed capital, expertise, and labor to a business, they can also be liabilities. The questions you need to ask yourself are:

☞ Will this person be a full and equal partner? In other words, are they able to carry their own weight? Make a full and fair assessment of your potential partner's personality. Going into business with someone who lacks a work ethic, or prefers giving directions to working in the trenches, can be a frustrating experience.

☞ What will they contribute to the business? For instance, a partner may bring in start-up money, facilities, or equipment. However, consider if this is enough of a reason to bring them on board. You may be able to get the same advantages in another way—for instance, renting a garage rather than working out of your partner's. Likewise, doubling skill sets does not always double productivity.

☞ Do they have any liabilities? For instance, if your prospective partner has declared bankruptcy in the past, this can hurt your collective venture's ability to get credit.

☞ Will the profits be able to sustain all the partners? Many start-up ventures do not turn profits immediately, and what little they do produce can be spread thin amongst many partners. Carefully work out the math.

Also bear in mind that going into business together can put a strain on even the best personal relationships. No matter whether it is family, friends, or strangers, keep everything very professional with written agreements regarding these investments. Get everything in writing, and be clear where obligations begin and end. "It's important to go into business with the right people," says Curtis. "If you don't—if it degrades into infighting and petty bickering—it can really go south quickly."

Incorporating. . . or Not

Think long and hard about incorporating. Starting a business often requires a fairly large—and risky—financial investment, which in turn exposes you to personal liability. Furthermore, as your business grows, so does your risk. Incorporating can help you shield yourself from this liability. However, it also has disadvantages.

To begin with, incorporating is not necessary for conducting professional transactions such as obtaining bank accounts and credit. You can do this as a sole proprietor, partnership, or simply by filing a DBA ("doing business as") statement with your local court (also known as "trading as" or an "assumed business name"). The DBA is an accounting entity that facilitates commerce and keeps your business' money separate from your own. However, the DBA does not shield you from responsibility if your business fails. It is entirely possible to ruin your credit, lose your house, and have your other assets seized in the unfortunate event of bankruptcy.

The purpose of incorporating is to shield yourself from personal financial liability. In case the worst happens, only the business' assets can be taken. However, this is not always the best solution. Check your local laws: Many states have laws that prevent a creditor from seizing a non-incorporated small business' assets in case of owner bankruptcy. If you are a corporation, however, the things you use to do business that are owned by the corporation—your office equipment, computers, restaurant refrigerators, and other essential equipment—may be seized by creditors, leaving you no way to work yourself out of debt. This is why it is imperative to consult with a lawyer.

There are other areas in which being a corporation can be an advantage, such as business insurance. Depending on your business needs, insurance can be for a variety of things: malpractice, against delivery failures or spoilage, or liability against defective products or accidents. Furthermore, it is easier to hire employees, obtain credit, and buy health insurance as an organization than as an individual. However, on the downside, corporations are subject to specific and strict laws concerning management and ownership. Again, you should consult with a knowledgeable legal expert.

Among the things you should discuss with your legal expert are the advantages and disadvantages of incorporating in your jurisdiction and which type of incorporation is best for you. The laws on liability and how much of your profit will be taken away in taxes vary widely by state and country. Generally, most small businesses owners opt for *limited liability companies* (LLCs), which gives them more control and a more flexible management structure. (Another possibility is a *limited liability partnership*, or *LLP*, which is especially useful for professionals such as doctors and lawyers.) Finally, there is the *corporation*, which is characterized by transferable ownerships shares, perpetual succession, and, of course, limited liability.

Most small businesses are sole proprietorships, partnerships, or privately-owned corporations. In the past, not many incorporated, since it was necessary to have multiple owners to start a corporation. However, this is changing, since it is now possible in many states for an individual to form a corporation. Note also that the form your business takes is usually not set in stone: A sole proprietorship or partnership can switch to become an LLC as it grows and the risks increase; furthermore, a successful LLC can raise capital by changing its structure to become a corporation and selling stock.

Legal Issues

Many other legal issues besides incorporating (or not) need to be addressed before you start your business. It is impossible to speak directly to every possible business need in this brief appendix, since regulations, licenses, and health and safety codes vary by industry and locality. A restaurant in Manhattan, for instance, has to deal not only with the usual issues such as health inspectors, the state liquor board, but obscure regulations such as New York City's cabaret laws, which prohibit dancing without a license in a place where alcohol is sold. An asbestos-abatement company, on the other hand, has a very different set of standards it has to abide by, including federal regulations. Researching applicable laws is part of starting up any business.

Part of being a wise business owner is knowing when you need help. There is software available for things like bookkeeping, business plans, and Web site creation, but generally, consulting with a knowledgeable professional—an accountant or a lawyer (or both)—is the smartest move. One of the most common mistakes is believing that just because you have expertise in the technical aspects of a certain field, you know all about running a business in that field. Whereas some people may balk at the expense, by suggesting the best way to deal with possible problems, as well as cutting through red tape and seeing possible pitfalls that you may not even have been aware of, such professionals usually more than make up for their cost. After all, they have far more experience at this than does a first-time business owner!

Financial

Another necessary first step in starting a business is obtaining a bank account. However, having the account is not as important as what you do with it. One of the most common problems with small businesses is undercapitalization—especially in brick-and-mortar businesses that sell or make something, rather than service-based businesses. The rule of thumb is that you should have access to money equal to your first year's anticipated profits, plus start-up expenses. (Note that this is not the same as having the money on hand—see the discussion on lines of credit, below.) For instance, if your annual rent, salaries, and equipment will cost $50,000 and you expect $25,000 worth of profit in your first year, you should have access to $75,000 worth of financing.

You need to decide what sort of financing you will need. Small business loans have both advantages and disadvantages. They can provide critical start-up credit, but in order to obtain one, your personal credit will need to be good, and you will, of course, have to pay them off with interest. In general, the more you and your partners put into the business yourselves, the more credit lenders will be willing to extend to you.

Equity can come from your own personal investment, either in cash or an equity loan on your home. You may also want to consider bringing on partners—at least limited financial partners—as a way to cover start-up costs.

It is also worth considering obtaining a line of credit instead of a loan. A loan is taken out all at once, but with a line of credit, you draw on the money as you need it. This both saves you interest payments and means that you have the money you need when you need it. Taking out too large of a loan can be worse than having no money at all! It just sits there collecting interest—or, worse, is spent on something utterly un-necessary—and then is not around when you need it most.

The first five years are the hardest for any business venture; your venture has about double the usual chance of closing in this time (1 out of 6, rather than 1 out of 12). You will probably have to tighten your belt at home, as well as work long hours and keep careful track of your business expenses. Be careful with your money. Do not take unnecessary risks, play it conservatively, and always keep some capital in reserve for emergencies. The hardest part of a new business, of course, is the learning curve of figuring out what, exactly, you need to do to make a profit, and so the best advice is to have plenty of savings—or a job to provide income—while you learn the ropes.

One thing you should not do is count on venture capitalists or "angel investors," that is, businesspeople who make a living investing on other businesses in the hopes that their equity in the company will increase in value. Venture capitalists have gotten something of a reputation as indiscriminate spendthrifts due to some poor choices made during the dot-com boom of the late 1990s, but the fact is that most do not take risks on unproven products. Rather, they are attracted to young companies that have the potential to become regional or national powerhouses and give better-than-average returns. Nor are venture capitalists are endless sources of money; rather, they are savvy businesspeople who are usually attracted to companies that have already experienced a measure of success. Therefore, it is better to rely on your own resources until you have proven your business will work.

Bookkeeping 101

The principles of double-entry bookkeeping have not changed much since its invention in the fifteenth century: one column records debits, and one records credits. The trick is *doing* it. As a small business owner, you need to be disciplined and meticulous at recording your finances. Thankfully, today there is software available that can do everything from tracking payables and receivables to running checks and generating reports.

Honestly ask yourself if you are the sort of person who does a good job keeping track of finances. If you are not, outsource to a bookkeeping company or hire someone to come in once or twice a week to enter invoices and generate checks for you. Also remember that if you have employees or even freelancers, you will have to file tax forms for them at the end of the year.

Another good idea is to have an accountant for your business to handle advice and taxes (federal, state, local, sales tax, etc.). In fact, consulting with an a certified public accountant is a good idea in general, since they are usually aware of laws and rules that you have never even heard of.

Finally, keep your personal and business accounting separate. If your business ever gets audited, the first thing the IRS looks for is personal expenses disguised as business expenses. A good accountant can help you to know what are legitimate business expenses. Everything you take from the business account, such as payroll and reimbursement, must be recorded and classified.

Being an Employer

Know your situation regarding employees. To begin with, if you have any employees, you will need an Employer Identification Number (EIN), also sometimes called a Federal Tax Identification Number. Getting an EIN is simple: You can fill out IRS form SS-4, or complete the process online at http://www.irs.gov.

Having employees carries other responsibilities and legalities with it. To begin with, you will need to pay payroll taxes (otherwise known as "withholding") to cover income tax, unemployment insurance, Social Security, and Medicare, as well as file W-2 and W-4 forms with the government. You will also be required to pay workman's compensation insurance, and will probably also want to find medical insurance. You are also required to abide by your state's nondiscrimination laws. Most states require you to post nondiscrimination and compensation notices in a public area.

Many employers are tempted to unofficially hire workers "off the books." This can have advantages, but can also mean entering a legal gray area. (Note, however, this is different from hiring freelancers, a temp employed by another company, or having a self-employed professional such as an accountant or bookkeeper come in occasionally to provide a service.) It is one thing to hire the neighbor's teenage son on a one-time basis to help you move some boxes, but quite another to have full-time workers working on a cash-and-carry basis. Regular wages must be noted in the accounts, and gaps may be questioned in the event of an audit. If the workers are injured on the job, you are not covered by workman's comp, and are thus vulnerable to lawsuits. If the workers you hired are not legal residents, you can also be liable for civil and criminal penalties. In general, it is best to keep your employees as above-board as possible.

Building a Business

Good business practices are essential to success. First off, do not overextend yourself. Be honest about what you can do and in what time frame. Secondly, be a responsible business owner. In general, if there is a problem, it is best to explain matters honestly to your clients than to leave them without word and wondering. In the former case, there is at least the possibility of salvaging your reputation and credibility.

Most business is still built by personal contacts and word of mouth. It is for this reason that maintaining your list of contacts is an essential practice. Even if a particular contact may not be useful at a particular moment, a future opportunity may present itself—or you may be able to send someone else to them. Networking, in other words, is as important when you are the boss as when you are looking for a job yourself. As the owner of a company, having a network means getting services on better terms, knowing where to go if you need help with a particular problem, or simply being in the right place at the right time to exploit an opportunity. Join professional organizations, the local Chamber of Commerce, clubs and community organizations, and learn to play golf. And remember—never burn a bridge.

Advertising is another way to build a business. Planning an ad campaign is not as difficult as you might think: You probably already know your media market and business community. The trick is applying it. Again, go with your instincts. If you never look twice at your local weekly, other people probably do not, either. If you are in a high-tourist area, though, local tourists maps might be a good way to leverage your marketing dollar. Ask other people in your area or market who have business similar to your own. Depending on your focus, you might want to consider everything from AM radio or local TV networks, to national trade publications, to hiring a PR firm for an all-out blitz. By thinking about these questions, you can spend your advertising dollars most effectively.

Nor should you underestimate the power of using the Internet to build your business. It is a very powerful tool for small businesses, potentially reaching vast numbers of people for relatively little outlay of money. Launching a Web site has become the modern equivalent of hanging out your shingle. Even if you are primarily a brick-and-mortar business, a Web presence can still be an invaluable tool—your store or offices will show up on Google searches, plus customers can find directions to visit you in person. Furthermore, the Internet offers the small-business owner many useful tools. Print and design services, order fulfillment, credit card processing, and networking—both personal and in terms of linking to other sites—are all available online. Web advertising can be useful, too, either by advertising on specialty sites that appeal to your audience, or by using services such as Google AdWords.

Amateurish print ads, TV commercials, and Web sites do not speak well of your business. Good media should be well-designed, well-edited, and well-put together. It need not, however, be expensive. Shop around and, again, use your network.

Flexibility is also important. "In general, a business must adapt to changing conditions, find new customers and find new products or services that customers need when the demand for their older products or services diminishes," says James Peck, a Long Island, New York, entrepreneur. In other words, if your original plan is not working out, or if demand falls, see if you can parlay your experience, skills, and physical plant into meeting other needs. People are not the only ones who can change their path in life; organizations can, too.

A Final Word

In business, as in other areas of life, the advice of more experienced people is essential. "I think it really takes three businesses until you know what you're doing," Drew Curtis confides. "I sure didn't know what I was doing the first time." Listen to what others have to say, no matter whether it is about your Web site or your business plan. One possible solution is seeking out a mentor, someone who has previously launched a successful venture in this field. In any case, before taking any step, ask as many people as many questions as you can. Good advice is invaluable.

Further Resources

American Independent Business Alliance

http://www.amiba.net

American Small Business League

http://www.asbl.com

IRS Small Business and Self-Employed One-Stop Resource

http://www.irs.gov/businesses/small/index.html

The Riley Guide: Steps in Starting Your Own Business

http://www.rileyguide.com/steps.html

Small Business Administration

http://www.sba.gov

Appendix B

Outfitting Yourself for Career Success

As you contemplate a career shift, the first component is to assess your interests. You need to figure out what makes you tick, since there is a far greater chance that you will enjoy and succeed in a career that taps into your passions, inclinations, natural abilities, and training. If you have a general idea of what your interests are, you at least know in which direction you want to travel. You may know you want to simply switch from one sort of nursing to another, or change your life entirely and pursue a dream you have always held. In this case, you can use a specific volume of The Field Guides to Finding a New Career to discover which position to target. If you are unsure of your direction you want to take, well, then the entire scope of the series is open to you! Browse through to see what appeals to you, and see if it matches with your experience and abilities.

The next step you should take is to make a list—do it once in writing—of the skills you have used in a position of responsibility that transfer to the field you are entering. People in charge of interviewing and hiring may well understand that the skills they are looking for in a new hire are used in other fields, but you must spell it out. Most job descriptions are partly a list of skills. Map your experience into that, and very early in your contacts with a prospective employer explicitly address how you acquired your relevant skills. Pick a relatively unimportant aspect of the job to be your ready answer for where you would look forward to learning within the organization, if this seems essentially correct. When you transfer into a field, softly acknowledge a weakness while relating your readiness to learn, but never lose sight of the value you offer both in your abilities and in the freshness of your perspective.

Energy and Experience

The second component in career-switching success is energy. When Jim Fulmer was 61, he found himself forced to close his piano-repair business. However, he was able to parlay his knowledge of music, pianos, and the musical instruments industry into another job as a sales representative for a large piano manufacturer, and quickly built up a clientele of musical-instrument retailers throughout the East Coast. Fulmer's experience highlights another essential lesson for career-changers: There are plenty of opportunities out there, but jobs will not come to you—especially the career-oriented, well-paying ones. You have to seek them out.

Jim Fulmer's case also illustrates another important point: Former training and experience can be a key to success. "Anyone who has to make a career change in any stage of life has to look at what skills they have acquired but may not be aware of," he says. After all, people can more easily change into careers similar to the ones they are leaving. Training and experience also let you enter with a greater level of seniority, provided you have the other necessary qualifications. For instance, a nurse who is already experienced with administering drugs and their benefits and drawbacks, and who is also graced with the personality and charisma to work with the public, can become a pharmaceutical company sales representative.

Unlock Your Network

The next step toward unlocking the perfect job is networking. The term may be overused, but the idea is as old as civilization. More than other animals, humans need one another. With the Internet and telephone, never in history has it been easier to form (or revive) these essential links. One does not have to gird oneself and attend reunion-type events (though for many this is a fine tactic)—but keep open to opportunities to meet people who may be friendly to you in your field. Ben Franklin understood the principal well—*Poor Richard's Almanac* is something of a treatise on the importance or cultivating what Franklin called "friendships" with benefactors. So follow in the steps of the founding fathers and make friends to get ahead. Remember: helping others feels good; it's often the receiving that gets a little tricky. If you know someone particularly well-connected in your field, consider tapping one or two less important connections first so that you make the most of the important one. As you proceed, keep your strengths foremost in your mind because the glue of commerce is mutual interest.

Eighty percent of job openings are *never advertised*, and, according to the U.S. Bureau of Labor statistics, more than half all employees landed their jobs through networking. Using your personal contacts is far more efficient and effective than trusting your résumé to the Web. On the Web, an employer needs to sort through tens of thousands—or millions—of résumés. When you direct your application to one potential employer, you are directing your inquiry to one person who already knows you. The personal touch is everything: Human beings are social animals, programmed to "read" body language; we are naturally inclined to trust those we meet in person, or who our friends and coworkers have recommended. While Web sites can be useful (for looking through help-wanted ads, for instance), expecting employers to pick you out of the slush pile is as effective as throwing your résumé into a black hole.

Do not send your résumé out just to make yourself feel like you're doing something. The proper way to go about things is to employ discipline and order, and then to apply your charm. Begin your networking efforts by making a list of people you can talk to: colleagues, coworkers, and supervisors, people you have had working relationship with, people from church, athletic teams, political organizations, or other community groups, friends, and relatives. You can expand your networking opportunities by following the suggestions in each chapter of the volumes. Your goal here is not so much to land a job as to expand your possibilities and knowledge: Though the people on your list may not be in the position to help you themselves, they might know someone who is. Meeting with them might also help you understand traits that matter and skills that are valued in the field in which you are interested. Even if the person is a potential employer, it is best to phrase your request as if you were seeking information: "You might not be able to help me, but do you know someone I could talk to who could tell me more about what it is like to work in this field?" Being hungry gives one impression, being desperate quite another.

Keep in mind that networking is a two-way street. If you meet someone who had an opening that is not right for you, but if you could recommend someone else, you have just added to your list two people who will be favorably disposed toward you in the future. Also, bear in mind that *you* can help people in *your* old field, thus adding to your own contacts list.

Networking is especially important to the self-employed or those who start their own businesses. Many people in this situation begin because they either recognize a potential market in a field that they are familiar with, or because full-time employment in this industry is no longer a possibility. Already being well-established in a field can help, but so can asking connections for potential work and generally making it known that you are ready, willing, and able to work. Working your professional connections, in many cases, is the *only* way to establish yourself. A free-lancer's network, in many cases, is like a spider's web. The spider casts out many strands, since he or she never knows which one might land the next meal.

Dial-Up Help

In general, it is better to call contacts directly than to e-mail them. E-mails are easy for busy people to ignore or overlook, even if they do not mean to. Explain your situation as briefly as possible (see the discussion of the "elevator speech"), and ask if you could meet briefly, either at their office or at a neutral place such as a café. (Be sure that you pay the bill in such a situation—it is a way of showing you appreciate their time and effort.) If you get someone's voicemail, give your "elevator speech" and then say you will call back in a few days to follow up—and then do so. If you reach your contact directly and they are too busy to speak or meet with you, make a definite appointment to call back at a later date. Be persistent, but not annoying.

Once you have arranged a meeting, prep yourself. Look at industry publications both in print and online, as well as news reports (here, GoogleNews, which lets you search through online news reports, can be very handy). Having up-to-date information on industry trends shows that you are dedicated, knowledgeable, and focused. Having specific questions on employers and requests for suggestions will set you apart from the rest of the job-hunting pack. Knowing the score—for instance, asking about the value of one sort of certification instead of another—pegs you as an "insider," rather than a dilettante, someone whose name is worth remembering and passing along to a potential employer.

Finally, set the right mood. Here, a little self-hypnosis goes a long way: Look at yourself in the mirror, and tell yourself that you are an enthusiastic, committed professional. Mood affects confidence and per-formance. Discipline your mind so you keep your perspective and self-respect. Nobody wants to hire someone who comes across as insincere, tells a sob story, or is still in the doldrums of having lost their previous job. At the end of any networking meeting, ask for someone else who might be able to help you in your journey to finding a position in this field, either with information or a potential job opening.

Get a Lift

When you meet with a contact in person (as well as when you run into anyone by chance who may be able to help you), you need an "elevator speech" (so-named because it should be short enough to be delivered during an elevator ride from a ground level to a high floor). This is a summary in which, in less than two minutes, you give them a clear impression of who you are, where you come from, your experience and goals, and why you are on the path you are on. The motto above Plato's Academy holds true: Know Thyself (this is where our Career Compasses and guides will help you). A long and rambling "elevator story" will get you nowhere. Furthermore, be positive: Neither a sad-sack story nor a tirade explaining how everything that went wrong in your old job is someone else's fault will get you anywhere. However, an honest explanation of a less-than-fortunate circumstance, such as a decline in business forcing an office closing, needing to change residence to a place where you are not qualified to work in order to further your spouse's career, or needing to work fewer hours in order to care for an ailing family member, is only honest.

An elevator speech should show 1) you know the business involved; 2) you know the company; 3) you are qualified (here, try to relate your education and work experience to the new situation); and 4) you are goal-oriented, dependable, and hardworking. Striking a balance is important; you want to sound eager, but not overeager. You also want to show a steady work experience, but not that you have been so narrowly focused that you cannot adjust. Most important is emphasizing what you can do for the company. You will be surprised how much information you can include in two minutes. Practice this speech in front of a mirror until you have the key points down perfectly. It should sound natural, and you should come across as friendly, confident, and assertive. Finally, remember eye contact! Good eye contact needs to be part of your presentation, as well as your everyday approach when meeting potential employers and leads.

Get Your Résumé Ready

Everyone knows what a résumé is, but how many of us have really thought about how to put one together? Perhaps no single part of the job search is subject to more anxiety—or myths and misunderstandings—than this 8 ½-by-11-inch sheet of paper.

On the one hand, it is perfectly all right for someone—especially in certain careers, such as academia—to have a résumé that is more than one page. On the other hand, you do not need to tell a future employer *everything*. Trim things down to the most relevant; for a 40-year-old to mention an internship from two decades ago is superfluous. Likewise, do not include irrelevant jobs, lest you seem like a professional career-changer.

Tailor your descriptions of your former employment to the particular position you are seeking. This is not to say you should lie, but do make your experience more appealing. If the job you're looking for involves supervising other people, say if you have done this in the past; if it involves specific knowledge or capabilities, mention that you possess these qualities. In general, try to make your past experience seem as similar to what you are seeking.

The standard advice is to put your Job Objective at the heading of the résumé. An alternative to this is a Professional Summary, which some recruiters and employers prefer. The difference is that a Job Objective mentions the position you are seeking, whereas a Professional Summary mentions your background (e.g. "Objective: To find a position as a sales representative in agribusiness machinery" versus "Experienced sales representative; strengths include background in agribusiness, as well as building team dynamics and market expansion"). Of course, it is easy to come up with two or three versions of the same document for different audiences.

The body of the résumé of an experienced worker varies a lot more than it does at the beginning of your career. You need not put your education or your job experience first; rather, your résumé should emphasize your strengths. If you have a master's degree in a related field, that might want to go before your unrelated job experience. Conversely, if too much education will harm you, you might want to bury that under the section on professional presentations you have given that show how good you are at communicating. If you are currently enrolled in a course or other professional development, be sure to note this (as well as your date of expected graduation). A résumé is a study of blurs, highlights, and jewels. You blur everything you must in order to fit the description of your experience to the job posting. You highlight what is relevant from each and any of your positions worth mentioning. The jewels are the little headers and such—craft them, since they are what is seen first.

You may also want to include professional organizations, work-related achievements, and special abilities, such as your fluency in a foreign language. Also mention your computer software qualifications and capabilities, especially if you are looking for work in a technological field or if you are an older job-seeker who might be perceived as behind the technology curve. Including your interests or family information might or might not be a good idea—no one really cares about your bridge club, and in fact they might worry that your marathon training might take away from your work commitments, but, on the other hand, mentioning your golf handicap or three children might be a good idea if your potential employer is an avid golfer or is a family woman herself.

You can either include your references or simply note, "References available upon request." However, be sure to ask your references' permission to use their names and alert them to the fact that they may be contacted before you include them on your résumé! Be sure to include name, organization, phone number, and e-mail address for each contact.

Today, word processors make it easy to format your résumé. However, beware of prepackaged résumé "wizards"—they do not make you stand out in the crowd. Feel free to strike out on your own, but remember the most important thing in formatting a résumé is consistency. Unless you have a background in typography, do not get too fancy. Finally, be sure to have someone (or several people!) read your résumé over for you.

For more information on résumé writing, check out Web sites such as http://www.resume.monster.com.

Craft Your Cover Letter

It is appropriate to include a cover letter with your résumé. A cover letter lets you convey extra information about yourself that does not fit or is not always appropriate in your résumé, such as why you are no longer working in your original field of employment. You can and should also mention the name of anyone who referred you to the job. You can go into some detail about the reason you are a great match, given the job description. Also address any questions that might be raised in the potential employer's mind (for instance, a gap in employment). Do not, however, ramble on. Your cover letter should stay focused on your goal: To offer a strong, positive impression of yourself and persuade the hiring manager that you are worth an interview. Your cover letter gives you a chance to stand out from the other applicants and sell yourself. In fact, according to a CareerBuilder.com survey, 23 percent of hiring managers say a candidate's ability to relate his or her experience to the job at hand is a top hiring consideration.

Even if you are not a great writer, you can still craft a positive yet concise cover letter in three paragraphs: An introduction containing the specifics of the job you are applying for; a summary of why you are a good fit for the position and what you can do for the company; and a closing with a request for an interview, contact information, and thanks. Remember to vary the structure and tone of your cover letter—do not begin every sentence with "I."

Ace Your Interview

In truth, your interview begins well before you arrive. Be sure to have read up well on the company and its industry. Use Web sites and magazines—http://www.hoovers.com offers free basic business information, and trade magazines deliver both information and a feel for the industries they cover. Also, do not neglect talking to people in your circle who might know about trends in the field. Leave enough time to digest the information so that you can give some independent thought to the company's history and prospects. You don't need to expert when you arrive to be interviewed; but you should be comfortable. The most important element of all is to be poised and relaxed during the interview itself. Preparation and practice can help a lot.

Be sure to develop well-thought-through answers to the following, typical interview openers and standard questsions.

☞ Tell me about yourself. (Do not complain about how unsatisfied you were in your former career, but give a brief summary of your applicable background and interest in the particular job area.) If there is a basis to it, emphasize how much you love to work and how you are a team player.

☞ Why do you want this job? (Speak from the brain, and the heart—of course you want the money, but say a little here about what you find interesting about the field and the company's role in it.)

☞ What makes you a good hire? (Remember here to connect the company's needs and your skill set. Ultimately, your selling points probably come down to one thing: you will make your employer money. You want the prospective hirer to see that your skills are valuable not to the world in general but to this specific company's bottom line. What can you do for them?)

☞ What led you to leave your last job? (If you were fired, still try say something positive, such as, "The business went through a challenging time, and some of the junior marketing people were let go.")

Practice answering these and other questions, and try to be genuinely positive about yourself, and patient with the process. Be secure but not cocky; don't be shy about forcing the focus now and then on positive contributions you have made in your working life—just be specific. As with the elevator speech, practice in front of the mirror.

A couple pleasantries are as natural a way as any to start the actual interview, but observe the interviewer closely for any cues to fall silent and formally begin. Answer directly; when in doubt, finish your phrase and look to the interviewer. Without taking command, you can always ask, "Is there more you would like to know?" Your attentiveness will convey respect. Let your personality show too—a positive attitude and a grounded sense of your abilities will go a long way to getting you considered. During the interview, keep your cell phone off and do not look at your watch. Toward the end of your meeting, you may be asked whether you have any questions. It is a good idea to have one or two in mind. A few examples follow:

☞ "What makes your company special in the field?"

☞ "What do you consider the hardest part of this position?"

☞ "Where are your greatest opportunities for growth?"

☞ "Do you know when you might need anything further from me?"

Leave discussion of terms for future conversations. Make a cordial, smooth exit.

Remember to Follow Up

Send a thank-you note. Employers surveyed by CareerBuilder.com in 2005 said it matters. About 15 percent said they would not hire someone who did not follow up with a thanks. And almost 33 percent would think less of a candidate. The form of the note does not much matter—if you know a manager's preference, use it. Otherwise, just be sure to follow up.

Winning an Offer

A job offer can feel like the culmination of a long and difficult struggle. So naturally, when you hear them, you may be tempted to jump at the offer. Don't. Once an employer wants you, he or she will usually give you a chance to consider the offer. This is the time to discuss terms of employment, such as vacation, overtime, and benefits. A little effort now can be well worth it in the future. Be sure to do a check of prevailing salaries for your field and area before signing on. Web sites for this include Payscale.com, Salary.com, and Salaryexpert.com. If you are thinking about asking for better or different terms from what the prospective employer offered, rest assured—that's how business gets done; and it may just burnish the positive impression you have already made.

Index